THE
PEAR TREE
PRINCIPLE

A SOLID GUIDELINE FROM
POVERTY TO WEALTH AND SUCCESS

By

Mary E. Schon

PAGE PUBLISHING, INC.
New York, NY

First originally published by Page Publishing, Inc. 2019

ISBN 978-1-64584-559-1 (Paperback)
ISBN 978-1-64584-561-4 (Digital)

Printed in the United States of America

I would like to dedicate this book to my wonderful family who has been patient with me through this entire process, namely my husband, Arthur, daughter, Marlise and granddaughter, Madison.

About the Author

B ringing valuable experience of over four decades, Mary Schon empowers the reader with the ingredients needed for ultimate success. She began her career with little or no resources, and now teaches others to climb the ladder of success, during which she has helped many achieve a "millionaire status."

She personally has owned and operated her own successful real estate brokerage firm since 1980, selling and managing millions of dollars' worth of real estate as well as building her own personal real estate portfolio.

In this book she explains sales brokerage, tax lien certificates, trustee and master commissioner sales, 1031 exchanges, as well as the art of creative financing and other real estate-related businesses that can increase one's income.

Mary has been awarded the designation of Realtor Emeritus by the National Association of Realtors in 2018 for over forty years of experience and service.

Her outside interests include playing the piano, watching performance of live plays and theatre, short trips, and being a mentor to Madison, her granddaughter.

CONTENTS

CHAPTER 1

THE STORY

Somewhere deep within each one of us lies the desire to achieve a particular goal or plateau at some point during our lifetime. Many of us know exactly what we want and have outlined steps or methods of how to achieve it. And then there are those of us who think we know what we want but have no real plan for obtaining it.

Many goals in life center around some type of achievement that has a financial reward. Most of us are profit-oriented and the potential for monetary remuneration is our reward for a successful game plan.

There is no shame in "profit" if it is made honestly and legally. In fact, it is the essence of the "American dream." The school system attempts to teach us to read, write, and do mathematics; however, an unfortunate fact is that most educators have no practical experience in *profit-making*. Most underpaid members of the learned staff are satisfied with their ten- or twenty-year status, and dedicated or not, they merely attempt to bring their students to a literate level. This is but a step on the stairway to financial independence.

Because of the economy, inflation, and lifestyles, our dollars do not stretch very far. Most of the time we struggle from payday to payday in hopes of some great miracle. We make the rent or house payment, the car payment, the doctor bill, the groceries, education for our children, numerous taxes, and insurance bills, and before long, it is all gobbled up. The ambiguity of dreams of a better way some time in the future must be replaced by a plan of action with definite goals and a timetable for their achievement. In order to change this dilemma, it is necessary to change our thinking. We must maintain a positive attitude. With determination and enthusiasm, we can move mountains.

Now, I am sure that you are thinking that *The Pear Tree Principle* is an odd title for this book, but let me assure you that this is the beginning of an extraordinary venture that shaped my life forever.

You see, many years ago, when I was a small child, there was this beautiful and lofty pear tree in our backyard. Most people would view it as a nuisance and a place for birds and squirrels to dine.

As a child of about nine years old, I'd often sit on the backstairs of our house and gaze up at that tree as I watched the pears mature and get ready for harvest. My grandmother would often take some of these delicious ripe pears and can them so they would, in a sense, last all year.

You see, we were very, very poor. Mom and Dad and I and my grandma all lived squeezed together in a very small five-hundred-square-feet bungalow. My dad was also supporting his widowed mother and his sister and her child. We survived on bare necessities. I knew I was poor when my grandmother sewed little dresses for me made from my dad's worn-out work shirts. We had a small garden and canned vegetables to last us through the winter. And although my mother worked, she was burdened with many hospital and doctor bills from serious surgeries that she had gone through.

Life was rough for us. I had no toys as other children, except for a little red wagon someone gave me. I had to go to other kids' homes and play with their toys and games, and sad to say, the kids at my school often made fun of me as I was not dressed as well, nor did I have the things in life they had. I became almost a recluse, not able to participate in the things other kids did. I became very shy and withdrawn.

I remember dreaming of having a swing set like the neighbor kids. Dad said it was not affordable, so he got an old tire and rope and tied it to a tree and told me that was my swing.

And for Christmas one year, all I got was one rubber bouncing ball. There were no charitable organizations back in those days to provide any help whatsoever. You just accepted the fact of poverty and tried to live with it best you can.

I was sooo skinny back then—only weighed thirty-seven pounds in the third grade.

My dad worked nights, and Mom worked days, and Grandma lived with us and watched me in between times. One day, as I sat there in my backyard looking up at that old pear tree, an astounding thought came over me.

I said to myself, "That pear tree can make me some money." The wheels in my head began spinning faster than lightning.

I picked up a few pears and saw how good they were—ripe, juicy, and tasteful. I put what I could in a few small market baskets and proceeded to climb and shake the tree so I could get more. I began filling many baskets and then loaded them into my little red wagon. I thought if Grandma liked them for canning and making pie, then other neighbor ladies would as well.

So with hope in my heart, I proceeded with my little red wagon and baskets of pears on a door-to-door sales effort.

Surprisingly, many of the ladies bought from me, and I felt this was the richest I had ever been. I went back to the tree and continued to get more pears until the tree was almost depleted for the season. I continued to sell, sell, and sell.

Now, I said to myself, "What can I do with this money as a reinvestment?" I thought and thought, and finally an idea hit me that was astounding. I felt I could use this money to create a new avenue and advance my little business plan.

So...I went to Woolworth's five-and-ten-dime store and saw the perfect idea for a new business venture.

There in the crafts department, I saw a loom and some colorful loops that could be woven into potholders. It was worth a try, and I was willing to invest my money to take the risk. So I purchased the loom and various colors of both cotton and nylon loops and began my potholder business.

I discovered I could combine various colors and designs of all types, and they were really very attractive and appealing. I would make them in sets of two and sell them accordingly. Remember, I was just a child but felt sales of this product was quite appealing to the ladies in my area. I started with known customers that bought pears from me and expanded these sales by asking if they had any relatives or friends that would like designer potholders. I also suggested they would make great gifts.

I sent samples of my work with my mother who showed them to people where she worked, and my orders were coming in. Each time I made a sale, I reinvested in more new loops and various colors. I also experimented with various designs.

This all started with that pear tree, and suddenly I realized… you could take almost anything and turn it into something.

So this is how the plan to erase poverty from my life evolved. I decided that never again would I want to be poor, deprived, and looked down upon. And it seemed like I was attracted to sales—but how could I ever know that sales would eventually shape my life into a full-time career?

CHAPTER 2

TRYING TO EARN MORE INCOME

I was now in late grade school, and I earned some money by babysitting little kids on my block. I also inherited an old piano from my grandparents and taught myself how to play it.

I learned enough to be able to play chords and soon found myself being asked by the pastor at my church to play organ music for two services a day. I would have done it for free, but he paid me approximately $40 per month.

High school was just around the corner, and I was about to meet new classmates and teachers. I was hoping to pull myself out of the rut I had been in during my earlier childhood. The school was small, and I liked all my teachers and newfound friends. My grades were always excellent as I wanted to excel and, of course, make my parents proud of me. I earned National Honor Society for all four years of high school, and I felt that I needed to continue earning somehow as my parents were still struggling.

After enrolling in school, I went downtown and applied for a job at a local movie theater. I was hired to work from 5:30 to 9:00 p.m. at the concession stand, popping and selling popcorn, pop, and candy.

Since I got out of school at 3:00 pm, I had time to kill, so I applied at a local florist downtown and got a job from 3:15 to 5:15 p.m. at $1.00 per hour.

I was now working two jobs, going to school, keeping my grades on honor roll status, and walking home (sometimes alone in the dark) after 9:00 p.m., and then doing homework before I went to bed. It was an exhausting schedule, but I kept it up for my entire four years of high school and worked even more in the summer months.

Upon graduation, I realized that neither myself nor my parents could afford to send me to college. We were still poor money-wise, and I had to look at my options.

Many of my friends found jobs, and of course, some had parents that could send them to college. I had neither. I decided that I must find a job and therefore started to comb the paper daily for "help wanted" ads.

I landed a job at Woolworth's dime store in the fabric department that summer, then later promoted to the record department, and finally a promotion to the head of all cashiers. In my heart, I knew I was capable of more, but I really needed a job.

I applied at the local newspaper, the *Omaha World-Herald*, and I was subsequently hired in the National Advertising Department. As it was now the end of summer, I decided to go to college at night and use some of my pay from my new job to finance my education.

Remember, there was no funds from parents, scholarships, or grants at this time. I therefore enrolled for six hours, which was half the time of a full-time student. I quit my job at Woolworth's and worked eight to five at the newspaper and took classes two evenings a week as half of a full-time college student. This was hard, as I had a responsible job with placing ads and keeping deadlines at my full-time job, and I had a lot of schoolwork and classes to attend in the remaining hours of the week. There was little or no time to socialize, but I was determined to fund my own education little by little.

I was still very shy and somewhat withdrawn, and I decided, although I was making progress with job and education, I didn't really like myself. I continued to feel inadequate. I read an ad in the paper about a Dale Carnegie course that could make changes in one's life. I decided to check it out and eventually signed up to take the class one night a week. It was the best class I had ever taken, as it brought me out of my shell and gave me confidence and enthusiasm.

Their slogan was "act enthusiastic and you'll be enthusiastic". And that it was! Slowly but surely, I was being transformed into a different person with different ideas and with new goals in mind. I felt myself more outgoing and with more confidence than I had ever felt.

At this point I was trying to decide what to do with my life— still living at home and going to college. I was now twenty years old and thought I would like to pursue a career in teaching elementary or secondary education when I was hit by a bombshell.

I received a call at work from my mother to come home quickly as my father had fallen ill, and she wanted me to take him to the hospital. When I got there, Dad had a violent headache, and his eyes were protruding almost out of their sockets.

I immediately packed him and Mom into the family car, as mom didn't drive, and we sped to St. Joseph Hospital where doctors said it was a serious brain issue and called in a brain surgeon. He said Dad had a lot of pressure on the brain and needed immediate surgery. The doctor called it blood clot on the brain; however, later we now call it an aneurysm.

The doctor removed a clot of one-inch thick and six inches in length off Dad's brain and gave him a fifty/fifty chance of survival as a vegetable. We were frantic and heartsick, as I was an only child, and Mom always depended on Dad for almost everything. Not only were we still very poor, but we were probably going to lose the rock of Gibraltar that held our family together.

After more than twenty-one days in the hospital and more clots forming in the brain, Dad passed away at age fifty-three. This, indeed, was the worst moment of my entire young life.

At this point, Mom depended on me for everything. And to make matters worse, the boy I had begun to date, Sonny, and was serious about, just left the week prior to Dad's death to the war in Vietnam for two years. So...I had no support at all at this moment in time—nothing but loss and grief.

I felt numb all over from this double whammy. My mom was also so grief-stricken, she could hardly function. I was all she had left, and she clung hard to me. I had to learn to handle all the family matters and finances, etc. I was the sole chauffeur and responsible caregiver. I did all the lawn mowing, grocery shopping, car maintenance, and you name it. Plus...I was still working full-time and going to college.

I kept thinking how long it would take me to finish at the rate I was going, so I took on another part-time job as a tax consultant at H&R Block. I was working forty hours a week at the newspaper, twenty-five to thirty hours a week as a tax consultant (during tax time), and still going two nights a week to college. I was a worn out rag, but I continued to save what little I could from both jobs.

CHAPTER 3

EXPLORING MY OPTIONS IN COLLEGE

During my time at the university, I started to take some elective classes, to fill in for my needed requirements, when I met a wonderful professor, Dr. G. Lewis, who headed the Real Estate Department. He taught many real estate classes, and I happened to be in a couple of them.

He said, "Mary, I know you are thinking of becoming a teacher, but you might want to consider real estate as a career and also as an investment."

I found what I was learning was fascinating and may possibly be that avenue to wealth that could stamp out my impoverished life. It made a lot of sense.

He encouraged me to take more classes and get a Nebraska Real Estate License. He also encouraged me to buy investment property.

I had no clue or training how to do any of this, but he kept encouraging me.

Going back to the Pear-Tree principle of making something happen from little or nothing...I decided to give it a try.

There were no real estate schools in my area in 1967, so I was told to read a very large and comprehensive book written by Robert Semenow and to memorize as much as possible. I was also informed that I must find a sponsor to be even able to take the test. The sponsor had to be a broker already, licensed, and in the business that would allow me to work under his license.

I started reading the book diligently and began to memorize all key and important materials. I wrote to the real estate commission and they sent me an application and further information on Nebraska License Law. I found a nice older gentleman who was a broker whose name was Mr. Rapp, who was willing to sponsor me, and when I finally felt a level of confidence, I scheduled to take the test.

The test was hard and contained a lot of questions, math and essay. The test took all day, and the results were that I passed with a 93 percent score. I was elated!

While still working at the newspaper, I was now a formally licensed realtor and could conduct business under a broker's supervision in the state of Nebraska. This was a sales license only. The next level up would be a broker's license, which of course would take more experience and additional education and testing.

At this point, I affiliated with a small, well-established company on a part-time basis.

I really didn't know much about the business, and there was no formal training program available at this old, established company. There were a lot of older near-retirement people working there, and most of them were not very motivated. I started by calling on people I knew and neighbors to see if anyone would sell. I got a few listings and sales but didn't know where to go from here. I realized it was a tough business to get into and make a success of.

I made some money but not enough to make a significant difference. However, I actually was doing more than some of the old realtors and some retirees that held their licenses at the company. A lot of them just came in every day to visit and drink their morning coffee.

I realized that if I were ever to do this full-time, I would have to affiliate with a larger company and probably one that would offer some training and help. Perhaps a company that had more notoriety.

However, any additional money that I made from this short venture was put into savings to build my small nest egg.

CHAPTER 4

LEARNING TO BUY REAL ESTATE

Before I got my real estate license, I had managed to save a whopping $3,000 from the time I graduated until I was twenty-two. I didn't want to spend it foolishly, and by no means did I want to lose it.

I began reading and scanning the weekly and Sunday Classified section of my local newspaper, looking for investment properties for sale, as Dr. Lewis told me to do.

My friends thought I was crazy and told me I should buy a new car with the money, but I didn't listen to them, as I knew cars depreciate. Instead, I continued looking to make a real estate purchase.

One Sunday, I saw an ad that caught my attention. It was an all-brick fourplex in a good local area, not far from where I already lived. The price was $26,000, and it was four separately metered townhouse style, two bedroom units with private entrances. It was like having four individual small homes, all attached together, and they had individual basements as well. This was less than $7,000 per unit.

I called the realtor who was an older, rather curt gentleman. He asked me how much money I had, and I told him only $3,000. He said, "You don't have enough money to buy it...don't waste my time."

I timidly said, "Sir, how much would it take?"

He said it would take $8,000 to assume the loan.

I could see that the property could make money by the income and the current expenses, but I was short by $5,000. I could not go to my "pear tree" for that kind of money...so I went to my widowed mom and begged her to loan me $5,000 with the promise to pay every dime back.

At first she said "no" and thought I was crazy. She had very little to go on herself, and that $5,000 was money left from Dad's life insurance policy. She said, "You have no experience and no one to help you run it. You will probably lose everything we both have."

I persisted...begging and begging until she couldn't stand my persistence and finally gave in. I called the realtor and engaged in a loan assumption with the $8,000 down and closed. I was never so scared in all my life. From the four units, it took two units to make the payment and taxes, one unit I could live in "free," and the fourth unit was pay-back-Mom money. Since I didn't immediately live free in the one unit, I enhanced my payments to Mom and also used some of the extra funds for upkeep and maintenance.

At this point, I learned many things managing it myself. I learned to be a bookkeeper, painter, lawn and snow person, leasing agent, complaint taker, etc. It was definitely a challenge.

Now, at this point, it started to go well and my philosophy became..."If you can do a thing once, you can do it twice. And if you can do a thing twice, you can make a habit of it."

So I felt that when I got my real estate license, I could find more properties on my own, as Dr. Lewis had told me.

After I got my real estate license, Sonny came back from Vietnam, and we renewed our relationship and finally got married in 1970. We then moved into the "free unit" of the fourplex (except for utilities) and continued to pay Mom off. We were able to save enough for our next venture which came within one year of our marriage. It was two duplexes for $28,000, on one lot. We had saved up the down payment and ended up buying and closing on it.

We kept working, both of us at the newspaper and with me still going to college and working my part-time job and the rentals. In 1972, after two years of marriage, we bought our own home and moved out of the fourplex. We then re-rented the unit we moved out of, which increased our cash flow and helped with our savings and our new home.

We continued to save and refinance what we had to make down payments on more rental properties. After four years of marriage, we had a child and eight rental units and, of course, our home. We had to go a little slower now, because the cost of raising a family, paying day care, car payments, and house payments can be overwhelming.

I kept thinking of how the "Pear Tree Principle" could influence our holdings, and then an opportunity presented itself from out of the blue.

Reading an ad in the daily paper was a private individual who had an eleven plex for sale. We called on it and met this nice old gentleman named George who wanted to sell, as he was getting older and wanted to retire. We didn't have an adequate down payment for an eleven plex, but we asked George if he would take one of the duplexes as a down payment. After an appraisal, we found out that each duplex was now worth around $25,000 instead of $14,000 (which was the original price we paid for each). George wanted $100,000 for the eleven plex, so we offered him one of our duplexes in exchange for the $25,000 down payment required to purchase his building. We got our bank to release one of the duplexes from the mortgage that was on both of them so we could convey it to George as our down payment on his eleven plex. We ended up closing and still owning one of the duplexes with the entire original mortgage on it. We now had seventeen units and continued saving and using our cash flow and inflation to continue to buy more rentals. We called it pyramiding our way to wealth.

And so, this is how I got from nothing but a "pear tree" to an ongoing venture of real estate acquisitions.

At our peak, we reached about three hundred rental units—basically starting with little or nothing—"Pear Tree Principle" at work!

CHAPTER 5

HOW TO START

I will tell you that most people would say that a good college education is the key to sure success. In some cases, that would be true, however, I can tell you that many people who do not have college degrees have also had extraordinary success. Success is nothing but failure turned inside out.

I ask you, what would you like to be successful at? What would make you happy and yet give you financial security and stability?

Most people work an hourly or salaried job and spend as much or more than they earn each month. One can never become wealthy by such means, and many people are heavy into credit card debt by following this path. It has been said that most Americans do not have any more than $1,200 in savings by the time they retire.

So how can we overcome this dilemma? How can you become wealthy or successful in view of all this?

Are you working a dull, go-nowhere job with nothing to look forward to? What are the necessary steps to change this cycle?

I go back again to the "Pear Tree Principle" where I have told you how to start small and with little or nothing and build a desired portfolio or empire.

Let's examine where you need to start.

No matter what your age or status in life, it is never too late to begin.

You must start with a plan. I will call it the right path or choice.

Now there are all kinds of paths, but just examine which one makes the most sense.

If you are thinking of opening a new business, statistics show us that most new businesses fail within the first two years. If you are thinking stock market or mutual funds, be aware that historically the stock market has been very volatile. You can earn it fast and lose it fast.

If you think safe CDs or money markets are the answer, be aware that your savings are eroding faster than the dollar you saved.

And certainly commodities are far too risky. So that leaves us with real estate, which in most cases has been the key to many people's fortune. Many millionaires have been created by investing in real estate, and you too can become one of them.

If you have little or no assets, you need to either build a savings for a possible acquisition or partner with someone (preferably a family member). If your boss gave you a recent raise, it is wise to set that aside every month and act like you don't have it, by putting it in an interest-bearing account. Next, you need to cut your monthly living costs. Look for sales in your stores and daily newspapers. Use coupons and giveaways. Give up expensive habits like smoking or alcohol. Shop for cheaper house and car insurance. Car pool to save on gas. Don't eat out frequently especially when you have to tip. Use all the extra money to build your savings for a real estate purchase. If you have a home with equity, I advise that you speak to your banker about establishing a line of credit (LOC) with that equity. Remember, you are not charged for it until you actually use it. You must have a sincere desire to set and achieve your goal. You need to weigh the odds, make the decision, and vow to commitment. You must contribute discipline, focus, consistency, perseverance, and enthusiasm. Remember, nothing great was ever achieved without enthusiasm.

When you have your little nest egg or line of credit set up, you need to start an investigation. Start by finding a good realtor, especially a realtor in your area that specializes in investment property. Remember that most residential realtors don't possess the expertise or the inventory for multi-family investment property. When you find one that you are comfortable with, have him or her show you and give you income-and-expense facts on the properties he or she present to you.

Also, take it upon yourself to drive the streets in areas that appeal to you, and check out properties not officially for sale in the market, and call owners directly to see if they would be interested in selling. Look for properties that appear to be vacant or some with yards overgrown or in a state of disrepair.

Go to commercial departments of several banks and meet loan officers, vice presidents, and presidents. Ask about rate, terms, etc. It is good to establish many banking relationships.

You are also best to talk to other landlords who can tell you the ins and outs of the business. You can and should learn a lot from other people. Remember, people are happy to tell you how they did it, and you can learn a lot from other people's successes and failures.

Most communities have a landlord association that you can join that has regular monthly meetings. You can meet a lot of people in the industry this way and learn much from them.

———•—◉—•———

"WALL OF CASH"

O nce you have found a property that you are interested in…that is, in a decent area and that makes sense, you need to figure out how to finance it. Whatever can be financed can be sold.

Most banks will loan 75 percent to 80 percent of purchase price or appraised value. This is called the loan-to-value ratio. That means that you need to come up with 20 percent to 25 percent of the price as your down payment. You may or may not have that kind of money for a down. But don't lose hope, as there are ways to accomplish this.

Some banks, if your credit and job history is good, will allow the seller to carry back 15 percent to 25 percent as a second mortgage or second deed of trust.

If you play your cards right, that means that you could possibly buy the property with nothing down or a very small down. You should analyze this thoroughly though, because now you need to make sure that this property with two mortgages will be able to amortize and support itself and pay all the debt service and related expenses and still have a cash flow. If it doesn't, you must evaluate the current rents to make sure there is room for further rent increase.

Remember, there are other expenses connected with the property such as the taxes, insurance, maintenance, possibly utilities, and trash removal, and you should also include a vacancy factor and a bad debt (collections) factor.

Only after all expenses are paid from the gross income, we have NOI (Net Operating Income). And after we pay all mortgages from the net, what is leftover is our CASH FLOW.

Now *cash flow* can go into your pocket, or you can use it to pay extra principal on the property, thus reducing the debt more quickly and building your equity position. I call this your "Wall of Cash."

It is wise to use this method of savings rather than to foolishly spend your cash flow on frivolous purchases.

If you do this regularly with discipline, you will not only pay the property off more quickly, but also, you will pay less interest to the lender.

One more point I would like to make is that, say for instance you had a 5 percent or 6 percent loan, you would actually be saving money at the rate of 5 percent or 6 percent or whatever the rate is at an interest rate that is greater than a bank CD rate.

Now…when you have several properties cash flowing, you can take a greater amount from each one and pool it all together and start paying off property number 1. This is your "Wall of Cash" build up. And as soon as property number 1 is paid off, even more cash flow comes into the equation from the free and clear property.

Each time you pay off a property with your "Wall of Cash," you gain more equity and develop even more cash flow to continue the plan to pay off additional properties.

I have done this many times, and it does work wonderfully, but you must be consistent and diligent in your effort, or you will be tempted to spend the money in other places.

Again, this is another example of continuing with the "Pear Tree Principle"—to use the little you have to increase your business from within your existing assets and resources.

In addition to all this, banks like you to pay off indebtedness quickly, and they usually open their doors more generously to you for future loans. This is also very good for your credit rating.

You should always try to maintain a high credit rating, which is your Beacon or FICO score, and to get rid of all your destructive debt.

There are two kinds of debt in this world. One is "constructive debt" (which are mortgages), because whatever is debt today will eventually become equity of the asset in the future.

Then there is "destructive debt," and that kind of debt is where people get into trouble the most. Let's say you bought a car. It started to lose value as soon as you drove it off the lot, although you still had a full lien to pay on it, and each year you owned it and paid for it, it was worth even less.

It's the same thing if you racked up a bunch of needless bills on your credit card at 18 percent to 21 percent interest...never building any value, but further increasing your indebtedness while the assets you bought or vacation you took were all a sad history. Try not making these mistakes. Take the right path in the beginning as there will be a time when cash flow will be in abundance and riches will allow you to pay for anything in cash down the road without debt.

It's smart to drive an older, paid-off vehicle with less taxes and no payment rather than putting on the ritz with a new vehicle with destructive debt. Using constructive debt and early principal pay down, you can build equity for future acquisitions in real estate.

I call each investment that is amortizing a pyramid...as it is "pyramiding your way to wealth"—again, an offshoot of the "Pear Tree Principle."

Also remember, the tenants' rents are paying the mortgages; it's not personally coming out of your pocket. Equity and monies are being earned even as you sleep at night. It is a business that you can operate while working your regular job, as you don't have any set hours to run it. And unlike other businesses, you don't have to keep regular hours, established employees, or worry about someone stealing money out of a cash register. Rents can be mailed directly to you, and you therefore have full control.

CHAPTER 7

RUNNING YOUR PROPERTY

You will be required to address maintenance issues from time to time, either personally or hiring it out. You should maintain an accurate set of books either by ledger or a computer program. You should also inspect your property frequently. Do not attempt to run it on "auto-pilot."

Make sure the grounds and halls are tidy and litter picked up. And try to screen tenants properly, as one bad egg can ruin the batch.

Prep each apartment, before renting, to the condition you yourself would expect if you personally were renting it.

Make everything clean, freshly painted, and in good repair prior to renting it out, and have an early walk through with the prospective tenant prior to surrendering the keys and signing the lease. Check each tenant's background from his application, verifying his current job and job history to credit and a possible criminal background check. Verify his income and talk to his former landlord, and check for any former evictions that he may have had. If the slate is clean, take him and have him sign a one- or two-year lease.

Upon renting to him, give him a tenant orientation list which are house rules that you expect him to comply with. A sample copy of such list is contained later in this book. Determine also if he has any pets and decide if you will have a pet policy or a no-pet policy. If you take the pet, be aware that the law provides that you can only charge up to 25 percent of a month's rent for a pet deposit. Be sure that the pet is not a threatening, aggressive pet such as a pit bull or rottweiler or a pet that would disturb or threaten any of the other tenants. Also, if you take the pet, demand that the pet owner cleans up after the pet on the grounds of the premises.

Remember too, that some people have service or companion pets and you are *not* allowed to collect a deposit on these types of animals.

Back in 1985, I established a program called Resident Search. What I had done was to take names of tenants from court records published in the daily legal newspaper that were being sued and evicted for wrongful detention of rent. This was very valuable in the sense that many of these people were habitual violators of non-payment of rent with various landlords. My program included the tenant's name, former landlord's name, date of eviction, and court case number.

I started not only using it myself for my own rentals but also selling a monthly subscription of the program to other landlords in the city. All they had to do was to call my office and give the name of the new tenant applicant, and we could immediately establish if they ever had an eviction in our county in the past. To date I have over 130,000 names of people to avoid in my community. Today I decided to provide the service free to any landlord that desires its use.

The actual plan to implement Resident Search is further illustrated in this book, if you wish to try to implement a similar program. This is another example of the "Pear Tree Principle" at work, whereby you can reap benefits from a program that you start with little or nothing and make a nice profit for yourself while you are helping others.

Once you start your rental business, it seems to get into your blood, and you can increase your holdings by continuing to pull equity out of your existing properties and make additional purchases.

One of my favorite board games as a kid was Monopoly. And the thought of doing this in real life definitely appealed to me.

An Example
Tenant Orientation
to Include
When Moving In
a
New Tenant

Tenant Orientation

Welcome to your new residence. Before you move in, we would like to establish some basic ground rules that are expected of you as a resident.

This is to ensure a good landlord-tenant relationship and to maintain a clean and pleasant surrounding for you and your neighbors. Therefore, we would like to review with you these expectations prior to your move-in as follows:

1. Rent is a priority both for you and for us. Rent is *due* on the first of the month, no matter what date you originally moved in. Any rent later than the fifth of the month, incurs an automatic 15 percent penalty.

2. You will be provided a set of keys for your apartment. You are *not allowed* to change your lock on your own. If there is a problem with your lock, you *must* contact this office for service. We further suggest that you have an additional key cut once you receive it; in case you are locked out. If you are locked out and then call our office, there is a $10 lock-out fee to be paid to the person letting you in.

3. Your apartment or house will be painted in white or neutral colors. You may *not* take it upon yourself to paint or change color or wallpaper the unit. It is what it "is" when you move in.

4. You may *not* put grease or food down your drains. Please use a grease can and dispose of it in the trash when full. You may not empty grease out onto the yard or premises either.

5. You may not put anything other than toilet paper down the stool. That includes sanitary napkins, diapers, paper towels, handy wipes, or any foreign objects.

6. Pets are generally not allowed. However, in certain isolated cases, there may be an exception. In such case, you are expected to clean up the area where your pet defecated. You may not sneak a pet into the unit unauthorized, nor may you care for, harbor, or keep a pet for any other person

(permanently or temporarily). Such will be a violation of your lease and can lead to eviction.

7. There is to be no smoking, eating, or loitering in hallways or laundry room, nor are children allowed to play in hallways or laundry area.

8. You are not allowed to cut or tear screens on windows or doors, nor willfully break windows. If you *or* a guest of yours engages in that behavior, *you* will be responsible for the cost.

9. Do not leave storm doors open or propped open for the wind to catch them. They tend to break when it gets windy, and you *will* be responsible.

10. You must *respect* the rights and enjoyment of the other residents, by not playing loud music or engaging in loud arguing or destructive behavior.

11. You must keep laundry doors closed. This prevents winter weather from coming in and freezing the pipes.

12. You may not touch or use or cause to be used any fire extinguishers in the hallways, unless a fire actually occurs.

13. If your building has a parking lot, you are entitled to only one parking space per unit. And...car must be operable. No junk cars or inoperable vehicles are allowed in the lot, nor may you work on cars mechanically in the parking lot. If you have any more than one car, any additional cars must be parked on the street.

14. You will be given clean or new carpet when you move in. You are not allowed to destroy it with grease, gum, red pop, marks from cigarettes, or irons. You are expected to vacuum it regularly and shampoo it or steam it on your own if it becomes soiled.

15. You are to report any maintenance issue or emergency immediately. Do not let it go...it only gets worse.

16. Do not attempt to light pilot lights on stoves or furnaces. Call the gas company immediately if pilot is out.

17. Do *not* install window-air units or take them out if they belong to the landlord. Always call our office.

18. Defrost refrigerator frequently if not a self-defrost.
19. *Do not* play plumber or electrician by messing with plumbing pipes, toilets, or electrical wires. Again, call our office.
20. If you live in a single family house, you must mow, weed, and water your own lawn and remove your own snow.
21. If your power is cut off by the electric company, you may *not* plug into the landlord's electricity in hall or basement. This is *stealing.*
22. You may *not* move any unauthorized people into the unit or transfer your unit to another person or persons without the knowledge and consent of your landlord.
23. You must clean the washer and dryer in the laundry room after your usage and dispose of your soapboxes and dryer sheets in proper receptacles.
24. You must put nothing other than trash and garbage in the dumpster and trash cans. No trash to be left on ground or in hallways, and no furniture or mattresses or tires are to be put into or around dumpster or on premises.
25. No outdoor barbeque grills are allowed on balconies, fire escapes, or inside of units. This is a violation of the fire code.
26. No storage of personal items are allowed on balconies, porches, fire escapes, or hallways. Keep all your personal things in your unit, or rent a storage locker.
27. If you previously had bedbugs or roaches in the apartment you are moving from, you must reveal that to us.
28. You may not engage in the use or sale of drugs on this premises. Anyone caught doing so will be immediately *evicted.*
29. You may not run a babysitting day care or any other business out of the unit.
30. You are to maintain your unit in a clean, respectable manner at all times and respect your neighbors' rights as well.
31. You *must* put your name on the mailbox, or the mailman will not deliver mail to you.

32. If you live in a building that has cluster mailboxes (which belong to the post office), there will be a deposit required by the US Post Office to obtain a key for that box. At this time, we believe it is approximately $42. However, such monies will be returned to you whenever you move and return key to the post office.

I HAVE THOROUGHLY BEEN ADVISED OF ALL THESE ISSUES AND HAVE READ AND UNDERSTOOD THESE RULES OF TENANCY AND AGREE AND CONSENT TO ABIDE BY THEM.

_____

_____

_____

_____

Dated _____

CHAPTER 8

LINE OF CREDIT

I found the best thing to do is to establish a line of credit. Remember, you do not have to pay a monthly fee or payment until you actually use it…which is a smart idea, unlike those who refinance and pull out cash in their hand and don't have a place to put it as yet.

You can also pay "all cash" for a property and beat out other offers who may be subject to placing a mortgage on a property (which will take additional time).

You can borrow on your line and pay it back anytime and continue the process repeatedly. There is no prepayment penalty, and generally, you are not asked what you are using the money for. It could be for a new acquisition or for capital improvements or whatever.

Let's take an example of a purchase by using this line of credit. Say for instance you have a $200,000 line of credit, and you use it to pay "all cash" for a property, and now you close and own it outright. Now let's say you do some minor or cosmetic work on the property and obtain a new generous appraisal of $250,000. Next, you go to a lender with your newly gotten $250,000 appraisal and ask for a new first mortgage on the property of 80 percent of loan-to-value ratio, which would equal $200,000. You now have enough money to pay off the line of credit again, maybe doing this multiple times, and thereby basically getting into these properties with technically nothing down, while still maintaining the line of credit as well.

It also gives you the power to make and complete the purchase more quickly than other people who would be competing for the same property, but would have to wait for bank financing, the appraisal, and loan committee approval.

Again…the "Pear Tree Principle" is at work, creating something from nothing again and again and enhancing your assets and equity positions. Isn't this just great? And as you repeat this time after time, you can even *increase* your line of credit and build your portfolio.

This process can immensely build and enhance your pyramid holdings and speed up your goals toward additional equity and wealth.

CHAPTER 9

WHAT SHOULD YOU PURCHASE?

So what do you think you should buy…single family, multifamily, commercial, industrial land, etc.? As a starter, you should start with something small…maybe a house, duplex, or fourplex. They all have their advantages and disadvantages. So in determining what to buy, it was clear to me that both multi-family and single family properties both had their pros and cons. Both could actually make good money if purchased right, but there is a clear difference in the operation of each.

Let's first examine the pros and cons of single family houses. When you purchase a single family unit and decide to rent it out, the pluses are that you can pass all the utilities and yard work (both lawn mowing and snow removal) to the tenant occupants. You can also concentrate and combine all your maintenance under one roof. And upon sale of the property in the future, you can appeal not only to an investor such as yourself, but also to single family home owner occupants.

This appeal to home owner occupants opens up the market to a greater number of buyers for you. These also can be appealing as a buy, fix up and flip for a profit. But remember, Uncle Sam's your partner in your profit when you sell. Although in the meantime, while you are waiting for a renter or a buyer, you will be absorbing the cost of the mortgage, taxes, insurance, utilities, yard work, maintenance etc., which can reduce your profits.

The disadvantage of a single family unit investment is that if it becomes vacant, you have a 100 percent vacancy factor which leaves nothing to cover expenses until a new renter is acquired. In examining multi-family properties, the pros consist of acquisition at a lower cost per unit than single family houses. It also benefits you when you have a vacancy. As an example, let's say you bought a fourplex and one unit becomes vacant. You now have a 25 percent vacancy factor, but you have 75 percent of the income to carry your mortgage and expenses until you re-rent the vacant unit.

One of the disadvantages is that you will probably end up doing the mowing and snow removal, but also you will need to provide service to clean the hallways and the laundry room as four or more tenants are not going to flip a coin to see who would love to do this chore. It is assumed you will provide all this, plus if it is not metered separately, you will be responsible for the utilities as well. And this type of property will generally appeal mostly to investors upon sale, and the buying pool will be limited.

It is very clear that the more units contained under one roof, the more beneficial to the investor to cover his operating expenses and debt service.

There are two kinds of apartment buildings—those that are built for the purpose and those that are conversions. A conversion is a house that originally was built as a single-family dwelling but remodeled and divided into more units such as a two-, three-, four-, five-, or six-family house. These types of buildings are generally less desirable (especially by banks) and require greater maintenance, as most of them are older structures and not equally conforming. They can be great money makers, as usually the cost per unit is low, but they may not always be in conformance to the local city code.

And you may want to know that if you or your spouse is a veteran, you can buy a one- to four-family property with nothing (zero) down. You must, however, agree to occupy a unit. Same is true if you are not a veteran and wish to go FHA financing. However, there is a small down payment required in that case around 3 to 3.5 percent down plus closing costs.

When you get to a fifth unit in a building, it is considered a commercial-type loan, and customarily it would require 20 to 25 percent down. There are cases where it may be permissible for a seller to carry back a second mortgage or deed of trust for 10,15, or 20 percent of the purchase price if it is agreeable with the seller and permissible by the lender. Most of these types of loans have a balloon clause of three, five or ten years, etc., as most sellers don't like to play banker for twenty years or more.

This helps soften the down payment for the buyer and may help the seller in obtaining a better price and terms for his property.

One thing you might want to keep in mind is that many sellers who carry back second positions may discount the mortgage for an early payoff. That's good news for you, as there aren't any banks who wish to discount the indebtedness you owe them. This also can put additional dollars in your pocket if you get the discount. Again, the "Pear Tree Principle" at work giving you some additional equity that you originally were not expecting.

Another thing you should know is that if the first mortgage or deed of trust is paid off, the second mortgage or deed of trust moves into first position and becomes a first mortgage or deed of trust. The only time this could be a problem is that if you decide to refinance the property and pay off the old first mortgage or deed of trust, you would be unable to put a new first on the property unless you originally put a subordination agreement into the second mortgage and note that has the former owner staying in a second position while you are putting a new first mortgage in place on the property.

And remember, if you default on the first mortgage, the person carrying the second can only keep his position during a foreclosure if he takes the property subject to your first mortgage. Otherwise, he is wiped out, and so is your first mortgage. In such case, the beneficiary (the bank) would end up with the property.

Some sellers may also want to carry the entire contract after a reasonable down payment. In other words, no bank is involved. The seller acts as the bank (or full lender). That is actually good for both of you. But this type of financing is getting to be very rare.

Generally, how this works is that you enter directly into a contract (purchase agreement) with the seller. You sign a promissory note for the indebtedness and a mortgage or land contract on the property is secured by the property itself. On a land contract, you will not get a deed at closing. Deed is held in escrow by an escrow agent or title company until the debt is repaid, at which time the seller instructs the title company to release the deed and have it recorded in your name. Prior to that, all you have is equitable title in the property.

Also, I will tell you that with any property you buy, you should have the tenants that occupy the property fill out and sign an "estoppel" agreement. This basically is information from the tenant that confirms what the seller has earlier provided. It asks the tenant to state his name, unit number, amount of rent, amount of security deposit, and expiration of his lease. The reason for this is that perhaps either intentionally or unintentionally, the seller may have given you inaccurate or false information, and it is wise to confirm the information with the tenants *before* you close on the property. This is just good business practice. You should verify everything that the seller or agent provided you with, and that includes taxes, utilities, insurance, maintenance costs and improvements, etc. No one will be a better "watch dog" over these items than you, as you will have to live with this property from here on after the closing. In addition, verify everything with the bank before closing, such as the mortgage rate, amortization, possible balloon clauses, due-on-sale clauses, and any other stipulations that may be favorable or unfavorable to you. These all should be discussed and verified with the lender *before* you close.

I have used both bank and seller financing in my career and both, over time, increased my equity in the properties. I actually love to have mortgages as I know down the road they all turn to equity faster than any other investment that I know of. Again…the "Pear Tree Principle" at work with tremendous amount of benefit.

THE PERFECT PURCHASING SCENARIO

In 2015, I got a call from my old friend, Scott W., from North Palm Beach, Florida, whom I haven't seen in many years. He moved from Omaha and retired with some capital that he wanted to use as an investment in real estate.

I was very surprised that he called me after more than thirty years, but he was responding to one of my properties I advertised on Loop Net (a national site I belong to that is similar to MLS, but is national rather than local).

Scott worked for me way back in 1980 as a sales agent and was fully familiar with multi-family investment properties, as he owned several smaller properties prior to his moving out of state. After they were sold, he invested in some single-family homes in Florida. But this time, Scott decided he wanted something bigger and was not able to find it in his area.

I told him about an *all-brick* twenty-three plex I had just put on the market and that there was a lot of room to increase current rents. The price was also below market with a lot of potential. After reviewing the income and expenses on the property, Scott made an offer to the owner and made a long trip up here to Omaha to physically view the property. They settled on a price of $586,500 which is approximately $25,500 per unit.

The property was in an excellent area in midtown and very desirous. I helped Scott find a lender to make him a first mortgage, and we asked the seller to carry back a second mortgage to lessen Scott's down payment. We then proceeded to close the transaction and help him secure property management, as he was still living out of state.

It was clear that the property could be worth more if rents were increased. So upon my advice, he instructed the management company to make some improvements and increase rents substantially. A few people moved, but most were willing to pay the higher rent.

Scott was very pleased, and as time went on, he realized that he had some phantom equity that could be used for another venture.

He asked my advice on what to do next. I told him that we could make another purchase if we could pull equity out of this property, so I began my next search on his behalf.

It took approximately 2.5 years to make the next move, but I found a *brick*, twelve plex in a beautiful area that I had sold to Mr. H. many years ago. I called Mr. H. and asked if he would consider selling for the right price, and he agreed.

I then sent Scott to a new lender who then ordered a new appraisal on his twenty-three plex, and lo and behold, we got an appraisal of $860,000 which was $37,391 per unit, which was more than enough to pull out cash equity to put down on the twelve plex without Scott having to come up with any other money of his own to close. I also advised him to contact the former owner of the twenty-three plex and ask him to discount the second mortgage he carried with him for an early payoff. The former owner agreed to this request, making the deal even better for Scott. He closed on the twelve plex and was now controlling a total of thirty-five units with no more invested than his original down on the twenty-three plex, less his discount from the former property owner who carried the second.

Can you see the "Pear Tree Principle" working here again? Getting a second building for *no money out of pocket*.

And for cases like this one and many others very similar, I have not only built my own pyramids, but also pyramids for other investors and clients such as Scott.

CHAPTER 10

AS YOU CONTINUE YOUR PURCHASE

There are some costs at closing, such as title insurance, termite inspection, building insurance, origination fees, taxes, and administrative costs. All these, of course, are write-offs your tax return. In addition, after you own the property, you may write off the real estate taxes, insurance, utility costs, trash removal, maintenance, mortgage interest, etc. However, one other benefit of buying real estate investment property is another write-off which never came out of your pocket, which is called depreciation.

Uncle Sam allows you to write off straight line depreciation over a 27.5-year period. You must first subtract the value of the land before you start, as land does not depreciate.

Let me give you an example: Let's say you bought a rental property for $220,000 and the land was worth $20,000. You would need to subtract the land value from the purchase and depreciate the $200,000 over a period of 27.5 years. That would equal $7,273 per year each, and every year for 27.5 years—write-off which *never* came out of your pocket.

This again is very favorable to our investment plan, for where else can you get that kind of a write-off? Also, your mortgage interest on your first and possibly your second mortgage (if you have one) is a write-off. It is possible that you could protect all the income from your rental property by write-offs and even have write-offs that extend into your other personal income from other sources, including your main job or occupation. More write-offs can also come from depreciation of appliances and capital improvements, such as a new roof, furnaces, air conditioners, new cabinetry, new concrete, etc. You can turn your investment into a gold mine if you play your cards right.

The best way to run your business is to cut costs and increase income. Look for opportunities in this area. When your property is highly productive and cash flowing nicely, you have also increased its overall value. Now…there are three things you can do. You can continue running it and build more equity, you can refinance and pull out tax-free cash (or establish a line of credit) that we talked about, or you can sell it for a hopeful profit.

Remember that when you sell, you will *always* have a partner to enjoin you in the profit. His name is Uncle Sam, and he likes to collect tax dollars from your profit in accordance with your tax bracket. You can, however, avoid or defer the gain for a while or for your lifetime if you wish. The procedure is called a 1031 exchange. This simply means that you would exchange your depreciated basis in the property for another property of like kind of greater value.

When you close on your sale, the money (proceeds) cannot touch your hand or your bank account. It must go into an account called a starker account which is held by a qualified intermediary. From the point of closing, you have forty-five days to identify another property you wish to purchase, and you have 180 days to close on it. The forty-five days is within the 180-day time frame.

The exchanger may list up to three properties of unlimited value, but if more than three properties are listed, their total aggregate fair market value may not exceed 200 percent of the aggregate fair market value of the relinquished property.

There is also a thing called a Reverse Exchange, whereby you have purchased a property *before* yours was sold. This is very complicated and far more expensive to implement than a regular exchange. You *must* have a qualified intermediary to handle this in your behalf.

After the exchange takes place, you now have a new, adjusted basis in the newly acquired property and will begin a new depreciation schedule. If you take depreciation during your ownership you must recapture the depreciation at the time of sale.

All these facets of real estate were so exciting to me that I love to educate people on how it all works. This is one true avenue that can definitely make you a millionaire or a multi-millionaire.

Remember that what we have been using to gain our wealth is leverage, and it is a tremendous tool. But...if used improperly, can be a double-edged sword. What I am trying to tell you is that we are using other people's money (by way of mortgages) to become wealthy. If we don't have a solid business plan and means to repay the debt, we could face a foreclosure, and not only lose the property, but we would also lose our down payment and any equity we had in the property. That is why we must be sure the properties' income covers all the mortgages and expenses and hopefully leaves us some reserves. It is a good idea to have reserves in case of a rainy day.

So...what could constitute a "rainy day"? Well, a market where there are a lot of vacancies or rent collection problems, extremely high interest rates, a major mechanical problem that could drain our reserves, or any other crisis that would take a lot of our capital. No one wants to face foreclosure; however, let me tell you that a bankruptcy will stop (at least temporarily) a foreclosure.

I see foreclosure happening more in single-family homeowner property than I do in multi-family property, as here we are looking solely to the homeowner for payment, whereby with multi-family, we have a number of tenants to look to for income in order to make our payments.

CHAPTER 11

BUILDING YOUR CREDIT

I t is most important that you pay your bills on time before they are due. This will immensely improve your credit score.

You will need good credit when applying for any business loan, investment loan, or personal loan. Banks like to make loans and open their doors to borrowers who pay back and pay back in a timely manner.

This is also important in establishing a line of credit which we talked about in an earlier chapter. Late payments and skipped payments can be the death and demise of your investment pursuits and your business. Every dollar you spend is borrowed, cash or credit, and when out-of-pocket exceeds your income, your upkeep will be your downfall.

Credit, according to Webster's Dictionary is "the favorable reputation derived from the confidence of others: honor, good opinion, founded on the belief of a man's veracity, integrity, abilities, and virtue."

Unfortunately, it's easy to spend next month's income before you earn it. It is said that one out of every six Americans has a problem with credit. There's more than $3 trillion in total personal debt in the United State, not to mention business debt. You should never use debt to live beyond your means and buy things you can't afford. A common phrase that's been around is "good debt feeds you (constructive debt) while bad debt bleeds you" (destructive debt). Bad debt would be vacations, luxury items, automobiles, and consumables that you purchase with outstanding balances, while good debt (constructive debt) would be mortgages or appreciating assets (such as fine art, collectibles, or some jewels). Mortgages which represent leverage is the greatest tool to build wealth. And without good credit, leverage is unobtainable. Leverage is the tool that expands your purchasing power and your success.

Your credit can always be improved whether it's new, poor, or excellent. So now is the time to make a solid commitment to improve your credit and overall financial health to become a credit millionaire.

You should always explore what credit is from the eyes of a lender. There are five factors in every lending decision. These five factors will open doors of a lender for you and they are character, conditions, capacity, capital, and collateral. Lenders consider the rate of delinquency as divided by your FICO score.

If your score is between	percent of time you will have a delinquency
0–499	85%
500–549	72%
550–599	52%
600–649	31%
650–699	15%
700–749	5%
750–799	2%
800–850	1%

CHAPTER 12

THE STEP-IN / STEP-OUT THEORY

N ow the "Pear Tree Principle" has taught me another means to acquire without much wherewithal.

I have personally developed this theory and have used it a few times in my career. I have never seen this theory presented in books or seminars, as it is very unique and must be used with much caution.

As an example, let's say that you wish to purchase a piece of property and you don't have the sufficient amount of money to put down—that is the traditional 20 to 25 percent cash requirement. Is there a way to make the acquisition without a down payment? Answer is—absolutely there is if the circumstances are right.

Let's say you find a seller who has either a house or investment property that is either free and clear or mostly clear and has a great deal of equity. And let's say he would sell it to you for $200,000, which would normally have you putting down 20 percent or $40,000. If you really want the property and don't have the $40,000 but do have a small amount of cash and a good credit score, you can try this theory if you can get the seller to go along with you.

First of all, let him know that you want to make a workable deal with him and offer to give him some financial consideration in good faith to start the process. Offer him a minimal amount of cash, let's say $3,000 to $5,000 in this example for him to add your name to his deed (This is called stepping in). Now he is not going to do this if you don't perform and fully buy him out at some point. Now he adds your name to his deed and such deed is recorded at the local courthouse and you sign a quitclaim deed back to him in the event you fail to perform. This deed is then held in escrow by a third disinterested party such as a title company or an attorney. At this point you are *temporarily* in the title with him in ownership of this property. You both must have absolute trust in each other.

Now…you proceed over to the lender and let the lender know you need to re-finance the property to buy your partner out. Now remember, as a refinance there is no requirement for a down payment. Down payments are only required on new purchases. But what you really need now is a high appraisal so you can get sufficient cash out to buy out your partner, the seller. Again…look for a very liberal appraiser. In this case it is wise to try for a $250,000 appraisal with bank giving you 80 percent of that figure or $200,000. After you close your re-finance at the bank, you pay the seller the $200,000 that you obtained in the refinance, and he deeds the balance of his remaining interest in the property to you (This is called stepping out). And he orders your quitclaim deed to come out of escrow and return it to you…as in this case you have performed. Had you not performed, he would retain your original deposit and ordered the quitclaim deed being held in escrow to be recorded and title would revert back to him in full.

But since you performed, you now have full ownership of the property with an in-place amortizing loan with the bank. Everybody wins, as seller got his property sold at an agreeable price, and you ended up buying it with a minimum cost out of your pocket (probably a few closing costs).

This will not work in every transaction, and you must have a willing, motivated seller that trusts you if he goes along with it. If you do perform and close, be sure the property will support itself and its amortization and expenses, as you are in a position of high leverage. Amortization comes from the Latin word *mortise* which means *death*. In this case it means the "death" or payoff of your loan.

It is also important that no matter what you buy, you should always have a cash reserve for the unexpected incidentals and surprises, as they come with the territory.

If you approach a seller with this idea and he backs away or declines the idea, go on to another and another until someone will accept and try this theory with you.

In other words, don't be a quitter at the first sign of opposition. By all means, always be honest and responsible in all your dealings, and you will gain trust and credibility. Do not dwell on failure or rejection as those traits will set you up for a sure failure. This is another typical example of the "Pear Tree Principle" at work—of getting a benefit without much input.

Example
of
Necessary
Documents Used
for the
Step-In/Step-Out
Transaction

REAL ESTATE FINANCING AGREEMENT

This agreement, made this _____ day of _____ 20____, betw
een_____ hereinafter referred
as PARTY A, and _____
_____, hereinafter referred to as PARTY B, is made in consider-
ation of the mutual agreements and promises of the PARTIES. The
agreement between the PARTIES is as follows:

DESCRIPTION OF THE REAL ESTATE:

PARTY B agrees to acquire and finance the real property located
at _____ which is legally described as _____
_____
_____
_____
_____
___ as surveyed, platted and recorded in _____
County, State of _____—including all structures, fixtures, and
equipment permanently attached to said real property in their cur-
rent condition. The PARTIES agree that the subject property must
be held in the current Portfolio of PARTY A.

Conveyance by Party A:

PARTY A states that they have good, valid, and marketable title,
in fee simple, and that conveyance by PARTY A to PARTY A and
PARTY B shall be, by general warranty deed, free and clear of liens,
defects, burdens, special taxes—levied or assessed, and encumbrances
whatsoever, except known city code violations (which Party B agrees
to accept). This conveyance, however, is subject to easements and
covenants now of record, including but not limited to utility ease-
ments not exceeding (10') in width abutting the boundary of the
real property and all building and use restrictions. In addition to the
general warranty deed that will be recorded, EACH PARTY shall
execute a quitclaim deed to the other party which shall be held in

Escrow by _____ located at _____
for the purpose of assuring compliance of this agreement by BOTH
PARTIES. The cost of the escrow services will be ($_____)
and will be the obligation of PARTY B.

FINANCING TERMS:

PARTIES agree that PARTY B will take possession of the premises
after the transfer of title to renovate, upgrade and improve the property in anticipation of re-financing the property. The property shall
be completed and refinanced within _____ days of
the transfer. Upon the refinance, PARTY B shall pay to PARTY A,
the sum of $ _____ and, PARTY A shall then in turn instruct the
Escrow Agent to release the quit-claim deed to PARTY B for its final
recording.

If the property is not refinanced by PARTY B within __ days as
agreed, PARTY B shall be deemed to be in default of this agreement.
Upon default, the property, including all improvements shall revert
back to PARTY A, and the Escrow agent holding the quitclaim deed,
shall, upon notice of default, file the quitclaim deed transferring title
back in its entirety back to PARTY A. Any improvements made to
the property will be at the expense of PARTY B and shall remain
on the property in the event of default to compensate as liquidated
damages as a result of the default. The Escrow agent shall NOT be
held responsible for damages due to the transfer of title NOT due to
their negligence.

TAXES AND INSURANCE AND INTEREST:

All real estate taxes & insurance & interest shall be paid by PARTY
A until full conveyance when PARTY A makes final quitclaim to
PARTY B. However, PARTY B, must pay and reimbursed PARTY
A, one twelfth (1/12) of the real Estate taxes, insurance and interest
for each thirty (30) day period between transfer of title and refinanc-

ing of the property. Interest to be charged at the rate of _____%
Payment shall be $_____.

COSTS:

Any costs such as appraisals, surveys, title insurance, termite inspec-
tions, documentary revenue stamps, escrow fees, or any miscella-
neous fees are to be paid by PARTY B.

ENTIRE AGREEMENT

This instrument constitutes the entire agreement between parties.
Neither party shall be bound by any terms, conditions, statements,
or representations, oral or written, not herein contained. Each party
hereby acknowledges that in executing this agreement he or she has
not been induced, persuaded or motivated by any promise or repre-
sentation made by the other party, unless expressly set forth herein.
All previous negotiations, preliminary instruments, and statements
by the parties or their representatives are merged in this instrument.

SIGNATURE AND EFFECTIVE DATE

This instrument shall not be effective as a contract until duly signed
by both parties. The date of execution and effective date of this agree-
ment is the date first herein above set forth.

BINDING EFFECT

This agreement shall be binding upon and inure to the bene-
fit of the PARTIES, their heirs, successors, assigns, and personal
representatives.

The undersigned PARTY B accepts the foregoing proposition on the
terms stated and agrees to perform all terms and conditions set forth.

Receipt and execution of this document is acknowledged this day of
_____ 20___. _____

_____

_____

PARTY (IES) B

ACCEPTANCE

The undersigned accepts the foregoing proposition on the terms stated
and agree to convey title to said property, deliver possession, and per-
form all the terms and conditions set forth herein and acknowledge
receipt of an executed copy of this agreement this _____ day of
_____ 20____. _____

_____

_____

PARTY (IES) A

CHAPTER 13

ESTABLISHING SOUND BANKING RELATIONSHIPS

I t is important to establish several banking relationships while you run your business of investing.

Get to know your bankers on a personal one-on-one basis. When shopping for a loan, talk to various lenders regarding terms, interest rates, balloons, call clauses, prepayment penalties, and length of amortization.

Banks will all vary in their requirements and stipulations. You should take the time to compare the differences.

All lenders will want collateral for the loan, and they will place their loan based upon the appraisal value of the real property or real estate being mortgaged.

Most lenders will loan up to 70 to 80 percent of appraised value or sale price upon engaging in the loan. Whether or not a lender will allow the buyer to engage in a second mortgage with a seller for part of the down payment is the lender's discretion. Know that what can be financed can be sold. Remember too, what is important is the note that you will sign. The note is what the lender can foreclose on and sue you for if the debt is unpaid, as it is the instrument of value. The mortgage is recorded at the court house, and the property itself is collateral for the indebtedness and security for the note.

If the loan goes into default and the property is sold at a trustee sale or master commissioners sale, the lender (who is the beneficiary) gets the property back. The property now goes into the lender's REO file (real estate owned file), and the lender will try to sell it directly or list it with a realtor. If the lender sells the property for less than what was owed to him, he can sue for a deficiency judgment against you.

If you sell on mortgage, deed of trust, or land contract and act as a lender, you may also sue the borrower on the note, even if you don't want the property, it can eventually create a lien on anything else the buyer has, to be used as the collateral.

If there is a balloon clause in your mortgage, the balance at time of balloon must be paid, or the balance refinanced. If there is a prepayment clause in your loan, you must pay the penalty before you can pay the property off. It is usually a sliding scale percentage established by the lender.

Most lenders have what is called a due-on-sale clause in their mortgage, which means you cannot sell the property without paying off the lender. As for instance, if you had a bank loan on a property and tried to sell it on a land contract to another party without paying off the bank, the bank (lender) can call the entire loan in as due and payable.

A lender cannot have both a prepayment penalty and a due-on-sale clause in his mortgage—which would be illegal. They simply cannot have their cake and eat it too.

Most adjustable rate loans will be based on an index, like the prime rate or the national cost of money or T bills. Most of them will have a floor (lowest rate can go down) and a ceiling (highest rate can go up). And you must pay attention to the verbiage in the loan documents.

For instance, back in 1977 my husband and I purchased a nine plex and obtained a variable rate loan at 10 percent interest from XYZ Savings & Loan. Consequently back then, rates automatically escalated all the way up to 17 percent, and we unfortunately paid it. This was a struggle, but all the other banks out there had high rates as well. Eventually rates were coming back down to the 9 and 10 percent level, but our rate at XYZ Savings & Loan remained at 17 percent.

I went into the bank to see Mr. Bruce B., president of XYZ Savings & Loan, and he said to me, "You obviously have not read the fine print in our document."

I said "what do you mean, Mr. B.?"

He went on to say that the note and mortgage said that they "may" increase rates according to the index and that they "may" decrease according to the same index.

I said to him, "This is what I understand." He then went on to say that "we *may*," not that "we *must.*"

I was devastated at his reply and decided to make a formal complaint to the Nebraska Banking Commission. They acknowledged my complaint as credible and started an investigation on XYZ Savings & Loan. Not only did they get them to reduce the rate back down to the current rate without charge, but investigated several other loans in their portfolio in order to reduce other customers' rates as well.

This to me resembled predatory lending on their behalf. But in the end, justice was served. Another thing that some lenders do illegally is "red-lining." There can be certain areas or types of properties lenders will refuse and decline to loan on. As an example, declining a loan in an area with crime or where bullets fly or a block or general area that has had some decline or deterioration.

It is therefore important that you must find honorable and sincere lenders in your area, or it can affect your investment business dramatically.

CHAPTER 14

RULE 72—RETURN ON INVESTMENT

I t is always a good idea to evaluate the return you will get on your investment, and therefore, I want to make you aware of a simple rule, which is the Rule 72. If you have never heard of it, pay close attention to what I am about to tell you.

All of us would like to double our money that we invest if possible, right? Well, Rule 72 shows you how long you would need to wait to double your money at any particular rate of interest.

For instance, if you are getting a rate of return on your investment of say 8 percent, you would divide 8 percent into 72, and that means it would take you nine years to double your money at 8 percent. Or say you were getting 12 percent return on your money, you would divide 12 into 72, and thus, it would take six years to double your money, and so on and so forth.

Here is a chart that you can follow to guide you in determining how quickly you can double your investment returns.

Rate of return	Number of years to double your investment
1%	72
2%	36
4%	18
5%	14.4
6%	12
7%	10.2
8%	9
10%	7.2
12%	6
18%	4
24%	3

It is important, therefore, that you select a property with a good rate of return (cap rate) or a property that you could easily convert to an attractive return by increasing income and decreasing expenses.

Cap rate is the rate of return on the specified investment. It is based on the net after all expenses are paid and the cash that is left afterward. Let's say a $200,000 property that nets $20,000 after all expenses has a cap rate of 10 percent. That's the net divided by the purchase price.

CHAPTER 15

FORTY-PLUS WAYS TO FINANCE REAL ESTATE

Whether you are buying property for yourself or if you are acting as a real estate agent for a client, here is a valuable list on how you can finance property:

1. Cash
2. Cash values in life insurance
3. Negotiable securities, such as stocks or bonds
4. Advance on buyer's future wages
5. Credit Union
6. Future bonuses that might be due
7. Loans or gifts from relatives
8. Secondary loans secured against real property
9. Blanket mortgage
10. Refinancing current property that one already owns
11. Personal loans using personal assets, such as jewelry, equipment, hobby collections, vehicles, etc., as collateral
12. Assignment of future rents
13. Passbook loans
14. Secure a business loan
15. Refinance automobile
16. Outright sale of assets to generate cash

17. Have builder or seller take a purchase money mortgage
18. Sweat equity
19. Use co-mortgagor or co-grantor to help qualify for maximum mortgage
20. Pledge or assignment of security
21. Compensating balances
22. Sales person or broker loans all or part of commission
23. Use contract of sale or contract of deed
24. If spouse is not working, have them take temporary employment until down payment has been raised
25. Finance personal property items included in sale separately from the home purchase
26. Private insurance plans for conventional loans
27. Income tax refunds
28. Christmas club funds
29. Special corporate financing for transferees
30. Pick up stock options and sell or refinance
31. Pledge dividends from stocks or other securities
32. Letters of credit from bank or individual
33. FHA Loans
34. VA—Veterans Administration loans
35. Savings and Loans Associations
36. Insurance companies
37. Savings banks
38. Private lending sources
39. Commercial banks
40. The Home Farm Loan Bank Association, for rural areas
41. Lease with option to buy
42. Step-in / step-out theory (mentioned in earlier chapter)

CHAPTER 16

BUYING AND FLIPPING PROPERTY

I t is always good to look for a bargain and buy low and sell high. There are many ways to find these properties. You may want to attend a Trustee or Master Commissioner's sale or acquire a property through a tax lien foreclosure. Another possibility is going to some of your local banks and ask if they have any properties in their REO files that they would sell at a reasonable price.

One more way of finding properties is to drive through neighborhoods and look for properties that appear to be abandoned or vacant and that look like they need work or attention. Many times a telltale sign is a yard that is over grown with weeds and grass that haven't been mowed, peeling paint, or snow that hasn't been shoveled. Or you may just talk to various neighbors in the area that interests you.

Another way to find properties which could be bargains is to check local newspapers for death notices, divorces, and bankruptcies, as these could be people motivated to sell at below market prices.

You could also check out short sales. That is where people are behind on their mortgage payments, and the lender would allow them to accept a lower price, just to get rid of the loan off their books.

Always try to estimate the cost of rehabbing the property, including the cost of holding in the interim between acquisition and the eventual sale. You will have costs of materials, labor, taxes, insurance, some utilities, yard and grounds maintenance, and mortgage or line of credit payment. Remember that for every dollar you spend, you should try to make three dollars. Plan too, your negotiations going into the deal as well as your exit.

Try to buy the worst conditioned property on the best block and also avoid crime areas—like areas where bullets fly, as these will be hard to exit from in the future. I have personally bought and sold and flipped many properties, but I had a very eye-awakening surprise a few years back when the IRS decided to audit me for five tax years.

It was a very grueling experience. It all started with a supposedly innocent phone call at my office from a gentleman who introduced himself as an agent of the IRS.

Now I always thought the IRS contacted you by mail, so I was surprised that this guy was calling me directly at my office.

He said, "Mrs. Schon, I understand you have a real estate business, and I'd like to stop by and see exactly how your business works. I told him I would not agree to meet with him unless my CPA who is Tom M. was present. He then agreed, and we set up a meeting."

What was to be one day of fact-finding ended up being a five-year audit that took approximately four months. I ended up giving him every receipt and every check I ever wrote out of the various accounts and entities I was involved in, along with all income from my investment property and income from all my real estate sales. I had bushels of paperwork I provided him, which was organized very diligently.

When he was finished with the audit, he threw everything in a big pile with no organization and said to me, "Mrs. Schon, I can't really find anything wrong with your files and paperwork, except I see you buy and flip houses and properties. And most years you have flipped five to eight properties."

I replied with a "yes sir."

Then he said to me, "If you buy and sell and flip more than two properties per year, you are considered a dealer in our opinion, and you must pay social security tax to the IRS." And so...he nailed me for a substantial amount.

Here again, I didn't know such a rule existed, so I want to pass this on to you to let you be aware that you could be required to pay social security tax on your flips. Remember too, there is a capital gain tax as well to be paid at the time of sale on the profit. So one question you should ask yourself is, is it better to sell and pay the capital gain and social security tax, or is it better to keep the property, fix it up, get a high appraisal, and pull out cash "tax-free" by a re-finance? You can then use the cash for the next venture without paying any tax at all.

Getting a high appraisal here is the key to pulling out more equity tax-free and perhaps using it for more acquisitions. Again... the "Pear Tree Principle" at work!

CHAPTER 17

THREE SERVICES YOU ARE GOING TO NEED

TITLE INSURANCE

With each purchase, it is necessary to secure title insurance. The cost of this is usually split between buyer and seller, 50/50. It is done in lieu of abstracting, which was a process used in the olden days whereby the seller's attorney would read and update the abstract, and the attorney of the buyer would review it for any and all title issues. There was no insurance for either party and only good as long as the attorneys were still alive.

Today there are companies that sell and insure the title for the buyer for the full length of time of ownership of the property, defending that title against any and all that would make claim against it. The cost is nominal, but well worth every penny. Herewith are twenty-one reasons why you should have title insurance on all of your holdings:

1. Forgery
2. Fraud in connection with the execution of documents
3. Undue influence on a grantor or executor
4. False impersonation by those purporting to be owners of the property

5. Incorrect representation of marital status of grantors
6. Undisclosed or missing heirs
7. Wills not properly probated
8. Mistaken interpretation of wills and trusts
9. Mental incompetence of grantors
10. Conveyance by a minor
11. Birth of heirs subsequent to the date of a will
12. Inadequate surveys
13. Incorrect legal descriptions
14. Non-delivery of deeds
15. Unsatisfied claims not shown on the record
16. Deeds executed under expired or false powers of attorney
17. Confusion due to similar or identical names
18. Dower or curtesy rights of ex-spouses or former owners
19. Clerical errors in recording legal documents
20. Incorrect indexing
21. Delivery of deeds after the death of a grantor

APPRAISERS

Speaking of appraisers, you will find some that are extremely liberal and generous and some that are very conservative. If you are buying a property, you want to find one that is conservative. This may be to your advantage in helping you buy the property for a lesser price.

On the other hand, if you are the seller or planning a refinance, you might want to find one that is very liberal and generous to give you the highest value for your property, as to give you the highest loan-to-value or cash out that you can get. Remember, an appraiser is only one man's opinion of the market at one moment in time. They are generally only good for six months. They are simply gauges for the lender as proof that they are putting out their money at a safe level to the borrower. And generally, bank auditors require that they be kept in the bank portfolio when they come for their annual examinations.

When an appraiser does the appraisal, he compares the subject property in three different ways. The first way is comparable sales of other properties that sold in the market. The second is replacement cost. In other words, what would it cost to replace the property stick by stick and brick by brick at today's prices plus the cost of the land. And the third approach to value would be the income approach (that is, if the property was used as a rental). In other words, the current income minus the expenses leaves a net income. When all three approaches to value are considered and combined, the appraiser arrives at a final value of the property.

Many times, you can offer other comparables that you know of in order to assist him. He gathers information from locally sold sales many times through the MLS or Loop Net. However, many times there are private sales that need to be investigated in order to establish a solid value.

PROPERTY INSURANCE

It will be necessary for you to secure and obtain an insurance binder upon closing on a piece of property. You will need fire and casualty as well as liability insurance. Be aware that there are two distinct types of insurance. The first is replacement cost, which is the most expensive and the one that most agents want to sell you. Upon stated loss, it replaces the entire property value stick by stick, brick by brick, less the deductible you choose.

The other type of insurance you could choose (which is less expensive, is actual value or sometimes called depreciated value insurance), which upon a loss will give you a depreciated value of the item or items that are insured—less the deductible again. As for instance a $10,000-roof with lifetime of twenty years is damaged at the tenth year of its life; thus paying you 50 percent or $5,000 less the deductible. Remember though that land does not depreciate in any case. So generally, I personally lean toward actual value insurance because it is less expensive and generally one does not lose the entire structure in a claim.

You should always compare premium costs with several companies on an apple-to-apple basis. Remember, the higher the deductible, the lower the premium will be. You should find a good company and an agent that will give you good service. Shop and compare before you decide.

CHAPTER 18

MY STORY OF AN ACTUAL FIRE CLAIM

Back in 2006, I had the largest and worst apartment fire that the city of Omaha, Nebraska, had experienced in twenty years.

It all happened around two in the morning when the fire department called my home to inform me that my beautiful twenty-three unit complex on the south side of town was on fire.

I was horrified to say the least, as this was one of my nicest complexes. Now this was a two-and-a-half story building that was all brick.

It seems that someone drug a mattress that was on fire out into the hallway on the second floor. Maybe someone had been smoking in bed, or perhaps this was an arson. I don't know, and the fire department didn't know either. All of our systems were in place including fire alarm, smoke detectors, auxiliary lighting, etc. The heat was so intense that it set off the fire alarm, and it rang until the fire finally melted it. Many people were asleep at 2:00 a.m., especially those on the top floor who woke up to thick smoke and flames and no way to escape. Several people were jumping out of top floor windows. Thirteen people went to the hospital, many with broken bones from the fall. Four people died in the fire from smoke inhalation. The story with photos was covered on all three TV Channels in the area along with coverage in the local newspaper. The coverage went on for over two weeks. Fire investigators were all over the property looking for clues, but no one could obtain answers.

We had actual value insurance with a $3 million liability attached to the policy. It is important to carry high liability on your policy if for no other reason than what I have just stated. If you wish, you can also carry an umbrella policy to attach to your regular current policy, which can expand your liability coverage.

The shell of the building was still standing and structurally sound. There was much smoke and water damage, and the insurance company paid a sufficient amount to cover damages and pay off the existing mortgage.

Instead of rehabbing the building, I sold the shell for a reasonable amount and paid off the current mortgage. Even though it was proven that we were not at fault or negligent in any way, we were sued by one family who lost two people in the fire. And here's where the liability part kicks in, and the insurance company provides legal first defense attorneys to represent you in court for this type of claim.

The insurance company wants this matter to go away outside the court room, so they generally try to settle outside of court if they can...which is what they did in this case.

We also had a rider on our policy which was a "loss of rents" clause, whereby the insurance company continues to pay rent on any destroyed units or any units that are out of service until they are in operation again. We had such a rider and did receive the "would be" rents until the sale of the structure.

There's also a separate rider to your policy if you have a boiler in your building. This will cover the cost of repair or replacement of a defective boiler. We have also had a couple of instances when we have had to use this rider when we had a boiler fail from a dry run.

If is important that you know about these extra riders you can attach to your policy and that you visit with your insurance agent for possibilities of any or all these types of happenings and any riders you feel would apply for overall protection and coverage that would be of value to you.

CHAPTER 19

EVICTIONS AND DEALING
WITH BAD TENANTS

There will be times when you may have to evict a tenant for wrongful detention of rent or there can be an eviction for misconduct or violation of any terms of the lease.

If I am evicting for nonpayment of rent, I usually act as my own attorney in court. It's not hard, but there are several steps to follow.

You must start by giving the tenant a three-day notice to pay or quit (meaning to move). An example three-day notice is included in this book. If the tenant fails or neglects to move within three days of your notice, you may begin an eviction proceeding.

This is called a "PRO-SE" eviction. In Latin that means *by self*.

I've previously written a booklet teaching people how to evict their own tenant without the time or expense of an attorney, and I provided necessary forms to file as the plaintiff. I generally charged $35 for this (another "Pear Tree Principle" way to make a few dollars, with little investment). This of course saves the plaintiff approximately $350 to $400 per eviction, which is the approximate fee an attorney would normally charge.

In my county, I can file a petition and praecipe (instructions to the constable) for as little as $46. I cannot, however, practice law and do this for other people without having a law license, but I can teach people how to do it for themselves.

I have done these eviction proceedings myself for years and have taught many people how to do the same for themselves. Attorneys don't like me for this, I am sure.

After the eviction and judgment, you may want to turn the evicted party into a collection agency, which is something I normally do. The agency will continue to pursue these people in your behalf and they will even garnish their wages—sending you a portion of their collection.

If you haven't yet sent the deadbeat into collections, you should issue him a 1099 at the end of the year to his last known or current address that he lives at. That way, the past-due rent will serve as additional income to him that he has not claimed on his tax return. Consequently, the IRS will then pursue him. And this will be a good lesson for him.

Other types of evictions which are not regarding collections of money are for violations of the lease, such as bad conduct, drug dealing, damages, unauthorized pets, etc.

In these cases, you must give a fourteen-day written notice to correct the situation, and if the tenant refuses or neglects, this is followed by a thirty-day notice to vacate the premises. This takes a different type of petition, and therefore, I normally turn these over to my attorney to handle.

From the process of evictions, I discovered another way to make money without much cost to me. I called it Resident Search. This program that I implemented was mentioned earlier in this book and can be an excellent avenue of additional revenue for you, should you wish to pursue it—another "Pear Tree Principle" way for you to make money.

CHAPTER 20

FORECLOSURES AND TAX LIEN CERTIFICATES

I f you would like to expand your business, plan to include mortgage foreclosures and tax lien certificate foreclosures. I will attempt to explain how all this works.

These are two different kinds of foreclosures. One is a mortgage that is unpaid by the borrower; the other is for foreclosure due to real estate taxes that were unpaid and foreclosed upon.

The mortgage foreclosure is when someone doesn't pay his mortgage and the lender gives proper notification of default to the borrower, and if the default is not cured in thirty days or time specified, the lender hires either a Trustee or Master Commissioner (generally an attorney) to advertise an upcoming sale in the local legal newspaper and to conduct a sale of the property on a specified date and place. If the original document signed by the borrower was a mortgage, the sale is called a Master Commissioner sale, and if the original instrument was a Deed of Trust, it is called a Trustee Sale. These are called third-party sales and are usually conducted at the local court house and is open to the general public for bid. The trustee will generally open the bidding with the beginning dollar amount required to pay off the lender, and his costs and further bidding is opened for anyone wishing to bid higher. If no one bids or buys the property, it goes back to the lender who is called the beneficiary and becomes his property as a REO (Real Estate Owned). The beneficiary may either sell directly or hire a realtor to list and sell the property to remove it from the beneficiary's portfolio.

If the property is sold at the foreclosure sale however, the act of foreclosure wipes out all other liens and mortgages except real estate taxes or an IRS lien. The IRS liens hang on for about 120 days and then disappear. The winning bidder gets what is called a "Trustee Deed" (Generally most lenders use deeds of trust rather than mortgages.)

The problem with this kind of foreclosure is that you usually never get to see the inside of the house before you buy it, and sometimes the former owner is still living there.

If the property is vacant, you cannot break in without a charge of trespass. Therefore, you usually cannot know the interior condition of the property. If you got it at a good price for the square footage and the area, you are probably taking a chance on the inside until you own it.

If the former owner is still living there, you may have to take steps to evict him, which could be a further problem. And sometimes these former owners are so angry that they lost the property that they can intentionally cause destruction and damage before finally leaving.

I remember a case of one I purchased where the seller was so mad that he took an ax and chopped up the cabinets, the woodwork, the air conditioner, and chopped a big hole in the roof. Luckily, the day I took title, I insured the house for all perils including vandalism. Fortunately, my insurance company covered the incident.

It is important that you immediately insure the property the moment you get the deed. You never know what can happen. Most of these kind of houses will need work to get them into shape to rent or re-sell. I have done this many times and can say that a person can actually make a good living at this.

If you are not lucky at the trustee sale, you can always call the lender (beneficiary) who got it back and see if he will sell it to you at a favorable price. It is vital that you insure it immediately, as I mentioned, and be sure to put new locks on the door.

You will probably have to de-junk it if there's any items from the former owner inside. Find a good employee or contractor to help you with refurbishing unless you are very handy and have time to do it yourself. Remember though, you cannot write off your own labor, but you may write off someone else's. Check all the vital components of the house. By that I mean the roof, furnace, plumbing, water heater, air conditioner, etc.

Make sure they are all in proper order before you start. If not, go ahead and replace them. Be aware that more modern kitchens and baths sell houses or attract renters. If you are stuck with old-fashioned cabinets, you're best to change out and modernize the kitchen along with new countertop, cabinets, faucets, etc. Everyone wants something new, attractive, clean, and modern. It's what sells! Remember it's a *visual feast*!

You can get top price or top rent if you follow this advice. One other thing that's important is the concrete on stairs, sidewalks, and driveways. Be sure these are not old, broken up, and present tripping factors. A nice lawn and landscape is also important as it adds to the attractiveness. Try to obtain $3 for every $1 you spend on these items.

You can definitely make significant money if you play your cards right. You should also be aware that the holding time on these can kill you and cut your profit. What I mean by that is, if you don't hurry the project along, you will be spending additional money to hold the property, such as additional utilities, taxes, lawn and grounds upkeep, and perhaps a few extra payments on your line of credit.

The other type of foreclosure is a foreclosure by tax lien sale. This is a little different because it has nothing to do with a mortgage or deed of trust. It is the local county taxing authority in your state that would hold the sale.

The sale generally happens once a year and can be conducted at your local court house or, as recently, online.

This involves people who have not paid their real estate taxes to the county treasurer. In my state of Nebraska, the certificates pay a healthy interest rate of 14 percent interest to the holder, and if the holder buys subsequent taxes over the next three years and the taxpayer does not redeem them, the owner of the certificate can apply for a Treasurer's Deed to the property, through foreclosure of the tax lien.

Again, the act of foreclosure wipes out any other liens or mortgages on the property except for the IRS.

I have acquired many houses by doing this. It also falls in line with the "Pear Tree Principle" by investing little of your own money (back taxes only) with return for huge gains. In other words, if you pay three years' taxes on the property, you get the property free and clear, or you get your money back plus 14 percent or more interest. How can you beat that?

For instance, I took a friend of mine, Bev, to a sale with me. It was a round-robin-bidding sale, which means parcels were offered to individual bidders in the room one at a time. If you were a bidder and it was offered to you, and you didn't want it, it was then offered to the person sitting next to you, and you wouldn't get another turn until everyone in the room was offered to bid. Anyway, Bev and I sat next to each other at the sale, and she was offered a tax certificate on a nice, brick, Tudor-style home with three bedrooms, formal dining room, fireplace, remodeled kitchen, etc. The home owner died and left a dysfunctional grownup son living in the home. He wasn't working and couldn't pay the taxes. Bev paid them for three years and then foreclosed as allowed by law. She had about $12,000 invested in the three-year period but wasn't paid off. Therefore, she foreclosed on the property and got a home worth over $175,000 for a mere $12,000 investment. And she owns it free and clear. Now she enjoyed this so much, she went on with the program and got two more houses and a vacant lot in an exclusive division which was worth around $55,000 and the two additional houses worth another $150,000. All this for a minimal investment in back taxes.

You never know when the "Pear Tree Principle" will kick in for you. Remember, each state conducts sales at different times and with different rules and different interest rates. Some states like Florida pay 18-percent interest, and Iowa pays 24 percent. You must check with your local county treasurer to find out where and when these sales will be held.

Many of the sales are now conducted online, but you need to check your particular state as to the time and process.

Even if you don't get the property, the interest rate alone is far more attractive than what a bank will pay. It's also safe, as it is local-government guaranteed. The taxpayer pays the county including the interest, and the county pays you back all your money plus the 14 percent or more interest. So you never see or deal with the taxpayer or current property owner personally.

CHAPTER 21

OBITUARIES, DIVORCES, AND BANKRUPTCIES

Another means of making large profits in real estate is to follow the obituary notices and the divorce and bankruptcies in your local legal newspaper.

You are wise to subscribe to the local legal newspaper. Here in Omaha, it's called the *Daily Record* and costs about $84 a year and tax deductible if used in business. That's only $6 per month, and what a value it is! It has everything that is legally happening in the city and county on a daily basis.

Here's, for instance, what it's done for myself and my partners: We started looking at the obituary section of the paper and noticed the names of the deceased along with the name of the law firm handling the estate and also the name and address of the personal representative designated. In one case we called a personal representative who said he represented six heirs of the deceased. According to him, they had a piece of land downtown which was about one-half acre in the industrial area. It was on the tax rolls for $24,000 value. We made a phone call to the rep, and he said they would sell for $20,000. I called my partner, Bill P., who I had been friends and partners with on many deals in the past.

Bill said, "Offer them $10,000 for it."

I teased him and said, "Bill, as stingy as you usually are, I'm surprised you didn't tell me to offer them a ridiculous $2,500."

Then he said, "Go ahead and offer $2,500 cash!"

I said, "You are kidding, right?"

He said, "I dare you—go ahead."

Feeling we had no chance at all, I offered the meager $2,500, and they shockingly took it. We held the property for a few years because there was a new stadium and ball park being built in the area and a rezoning was taking place. The wheels began to spin, and we thought the property might be of some value to someone in that location should we decide to sell it. All we were doing was mowing the grass and paying taxes anyway on this vacant piece of ground. So Bill and I finally decided that we would see what we could get for it. Then, suddenly after putting up a large "For Sale" sign in front of it, we sold it to a local developer for $295,000!

Now that's a windfall that's almost unbelievable! Again, going in with little investment and gaining a lot is our "Pear Tree Principle" at work again. You have to be able to know who is and who is not motivated to sell. Cases of death, divorce, and bankruptcy are generally motivated people.

Either call on them yourself and put the personal touch to work, or have an employee, partner, or associate call in your behalf. You can also run ads in the daily paper stating that you buy houses or put up signs in various areas with your phone number stating "I/We buy houses" inviting people to call you.

Repeat any successful performances that you make in any of the areas I have designated. You must put forth effort and persevere in order to make things happen. Good fortune and success will not simply drop in your lap.

Investigate all the possibilities and talk to other people who have successfully tried them. Opportunities are everywhere you go. You just have to seek them out. Whether you go alone or with a partner, it's best to do something rather than nothing.

And as you progress in achieving your goals and dreams, it is very wise to read all the self-help books and real estate investment books that you can get your hands on. One I like really well is Napoleon Hill's *Think and Grow Rich*.

These are people who have already experienced success and give you avenues on how to achieve it. So if you feel you are poor or just living paycheck to paycheck, you owe it to yourself to try some of the principles established in this book as they are tried, true, and sound.

Every experience makes you and your partners or customers more seasoned as investors. Remember visualization is vital. You must visualize how you will succeed and where you would like to be five, ten, or fifteen years from now. Would you be planning for your retirement, a college education for your children, or just discretionary money for things you would like in life? Whatever your focus or goal is, visualize, focus, and do not and I repeat *do not deviate* from it.

OBSTACLES

There are many things and distractions that prevent people from reaching their goals. So I ask you, "Where do you spend your time?"

If you are like a lot of people, you may spend hours in front of your TV set or on a computer or movie shows or at sports events and doing out-of-control spending and shopping in stores or over the internet. These are *all* time wasters, as they will take up your valuable time and give you little or nothing in return. Spending weeks and years on an unfulfilling job is also a time waster. Many people do not enjoy what they do, but become a victim of circumstances, which also is a time waster.

Time is very precious and ill-spent time can also lead to failure. Therefore, until you are independently wealthy, use your time well in planning and organization and with an outlined strategy that I have suggested in this book.

Rome was not built in a day, a week, or a year, and neither is your real estate investment career. It takes time, patience, careful planning, dedication, without interruptions or distractions.

Take on the attitude of winning, and by all means *do not* procrastinate, as it is a sure setup for doom and failure.

What Is Success?

Remember this...success is nothing but failure turned inside out. No one really plans to fail, but most fail to plan.

So what should you do on your way up the ladder to success? Well, here's what I noticed on my success ladder:

As I was growing my business and my portfolio, I noticed something very astounding along the way. This is a vital secret to ongoing, continual success.

You see, when we receive profit, good fortune, and success, and feel we are on top of the world...remember that a lot of people are not as fortunate and many of them are struggling just to make it day to day.

So...as a good gesture and in genuine thankfulness of our success, it has been my personal experience that those who give back something to a charity, community, or a church or helping organization, seem to have continual success and blessings a hundred fold. It seems to be a natural rule of nature and universal mankind. Besides, it's a good feeling to be able to help someone less fortunate than ourselves.

CHAPTER 22

OTHER THINGS TO CONSIDER

To Control or Not Control Your Property by Using Property Management Companies

I f you are currently busy in another full-time occupation, you might feel you don't have the time to control or watch over your rental properties. In such case, you may have to hire a property management company to oversee your properties. Although the cost of their services are tax deductible, remember the added cost of 6 to 10 percent or more of the income will definitely reduce your cash flow. And most companies will have you sign a one-year agreement, and they generally also take one-half the amount of rent on a new rental in addition to their percentage, and most also upcharge for materials and maintenance.

Using a management company can make sense if you live out of the area or out of state. But if you are living in the same city or near your properties, I would suggest you regularly check on your management company and your monthly statements from them. I have found many of them to be unprincipled and some that are not competent.

I recently ran into a company that does not even show your vacant units. They put a digital lock box on the vacant unit's door and tell the prospective tenant to go over there and show it to himself. This is the height of laziness. Do you realize that the prospective tenant could go in and damage the premises, party, illegally move himself in, or steal the appliances? This is why you must ask all necessary questions to your management company as to how they conduct business and what you can expect from their services.

Some management companies also write a clause in their contract giving themselves the exclusive right to list your property with them should you decide to sell. You should be able, at the time of sale, to select whoever you wish to market your property.

You should also always check your monthly statements from them for errors or overcharges in time or materials.

Backing Up Your System

If you are seriously thinking of making a continual investment in real estate that you personally would be running and controlling, then I need to tell you…the bigger you build your company and your volume, the more you will need backup. It will be difficult, if not impossible, to do everything yourself. Although you will be wearing many hats, you will definitely have your hands full.

Once you have acquired the unit or units, you will need to go through the process of screening, collecting deposits and rents, drawing up application forms, leases, and making deposits in a local bank, paying the mortgage, insurance, taxes, vendors, utilities, and handling employees and independent contractors. You will also have to deal with emergency and routine maintenance calls such as plumbers, carpenters, electricians, heating HVAC technicians, exterminators, etc. You will need to have qualified people in place to handle all of these issues if you are not doing them yourself.

Also, if you want to leave town or take a vacation or time off, you need a replacement for yourself in case your tenants have an emergency in your absence. If, however, you have employees, you will also need to set up payroll, withholding, workman's compensation insurance, IRA plans, insurance, and pensions.

You should also have emergency technicians for any after-hour problems or emergencies. Every business system needs backup in all areas, whether it's a family member or a hired employee, you need to have someone in place in all areas, less your business declines or fails. You must also have workman's compensation insurance and liability insurance in case a tenant or employee should be injured or killed on your property during their employment or residency. Accidents do happen, and usually unexpectedly. You should also carry insurance for employee dishonesty. There are situations whereby your help can embezzle or steal from you or your company or from those you serve. Backup and coverage are so important if you are going to be in business.

CHAPTER 23

ALL ABOUT TICS
TENANTS IN COMMON

There is also the case of properties being bought and held in a TIC (Tenants in Common). This is a passive type of investment and generally offered only to accredited investors by prospectus. An accredited investor is defined as one who has assets and/or income in excess of $250,000.

The properties offered are generally large projects that are multi-million dollar in price and are owned by multiple investors. There is a limit of no more than thirty-six investors in any one given TIC. I have personally invested in several of them, and I will tell you that some are good and others are not. The properties are introduced by a national sponsor who generally puts out a prospectus which outlines benefits and risks.

Many people use them when they have sold a local property and can't find a 1031 exchange property to purchase for the exchange, so they turn to doing a TIC which qualifies as a 1031 property for purchase. Of course, you can buy into one even if you are not exchanging.

You receive deed for your share or interest in the project, but you have no active participation or control of the project, as the sponsor generally manages it or hires a separate professional management company to oversee it.

Each project/property has an estimated return to the investors, but it is not guaranteed. Generally, each investor makes a minimum or more than minimum investment, and the sponsor obtains a bank loan for the balance of the acquisition for the entire group that is investing in it. Such loan is generally a non-recourse type loan, which means in the event of default, no investor is personally liable on the loan. The problem with this kind of investment is that there is "no exit" for the individual investors and also "no control", as it is a passive investment. One must wait until the group or manager/sponsor decides to sell before you can exit. There is no secondary market that I am aware of as of this writing. Many people like these because there is no personal responsibility on behalf of the investors and you can generally just go to your mailbox once a month and get a check and not be personally involved.

Many of these projects involve apartment buildings, shopping centers, office buildings, medical centers, industrial properties, assisted-living centers, student housing, etc. I have both made and lost money in these ventures and would warn you to be extremely careful and look at all aspects of the deal while diligently reviewing the prospectus.

There is a lot of paperwork involved as well as a lot of group conference calls to make on-going decisions between members of the group and the sponsors.

CHAPTER 24

GETTING A REAL ESTATE LICENSE

When I was twenty-two, I did take Professor Lewis's advice and decided to get my real estate license. This is a good thing to have if you are an investor, as you can get some of the commission on listed properties that you may want to purchase. I found this to be most beneficial as this reduced my cost in the property. In addition, on the properties that I didn't buy, I was able to sell them to other investors and collect further commissions which I was able to set aside for further down payments and acquisitions of my own. In other words, the income from commissions can be significant and give you a jump start for down payments on more properties. Again, the "Pear Tree Principle" is at work when you figure that you can start with nothing and obtain a listing by personal contact and work it and find a buyer and actually get paid 5 to 7 percent of the purchase price.

Back when I first got my license, I really didn't know what to do. As I said before, it appeared to be a hard business to break into if I were to make a full-time living at it. I was still working at the newspaper full-time and working part-time for a small real estate firm, making some small sales from people I knew. One day my boss at the newspaper called me in and said, "Mary, I understand you are selling real estate on the side."

I said, "Yes, Mac."

He said, "We don't take too well to this around here. Which job is it going to be? That job or this job?"

It was almost like a threat. I proceeded to tell him that I was doing real estate after 5:00 p.m. and weekends on my own time. He said it didn't matter and that I better make up my mind.

It was about that time that a friend of mine, Dale H., was working at a larger company called Real Estate Associates, and I mentioned to him what I was being put through. Before I knew it, one of the owners of the company called me and asked if I'd like to come over and join their firm full-time.

I interviewed with him, and he hired me. I then walked into Mac's office and gave him my two-week notice.

Mac said, "Why? You can't quit, Mary."

I said to him, "You asked me which job I wanted, and I have chosen the other job." I knew instantly that he tried to intimidate me, but I had made up my mind. He knew I was good at what I did at the newspaper, and he would find it hard to replace me. He actually wanted me to stay and imprison myself to the company for rather small wages.

So…after two weeks I walked out the door of a job I held for fourteen years, and with tears in my eyes and hope in my heart, I headed to the parking lot to get into my car and never looked back.

I was to start my new career at RE Associates on Monday and really didn't know what to expect. When I arrived, everyone seemed nice and greeted me with a warm welcome. Mr. Kerwin, who hired me, showed me around and directed me to my new desk and cubicle. It was kind of an individual area with partitions. He was very nice to me and showed me the entire office, break room, etc. After showing me around and introducing me to everyone, including all the secretaries, agents, and closing personnel, he pointed to my desk, a phone book, and said, "Now you can get started."

I looked around and hoped I didn't appear to be too foolish but asked, "What should I do now?"

He said, "Make some contacts and get some listings." After he said that, he said, "Remember, to list is to last." Frankly, I didn't know who to call or what to do. The business I had done part-time at the other very small real estate firm was basically business I developed by acquaintances and neighbors. And now I was swimming with the big fish. Suddenly I felt, perhaps, I had made a mistake quitting my fourteen-year job at the newspaper.

I now have *no income,* and I have exhausted all the people and friends I knew that bought from me when I was at the small real estate firm. I was beginning to get scared, as I had bills and mortgage on my home, car payments, and child care for my three-year-old daughter.

I asked Mr. Kerwin who I should contact. He said to call on FSBOs (For Sale by Owners) and expired listings. He also said that there were training tapes I could watch and listen to, which I began immediately.

I picked up the phone and started calling FSBOs which I saw in the local newspaper, without exception, either another realtor landed the listing, or the home owner would tell me he was planning on saving the commission by selling it himself.

I called on some expired listings, but again, most were already contacted by another realtor or were already relisted. Remember, there are about two-thousand-plus realtors who operate through the MLS in my community, and most were more experienced than I was. I felt I didn't have a chance. But later, I realized out of that number only about 20 percent of them actually worked and made a living.

I went back to Mr. Kerwin, and he said to go out to a nearby neighborhood and knock on doors in an area close to the office and ask people if they wanted to sell. He called it farming an area. It was now end of November, and it was cold outside, but I went out and began knocking on doors. In most cases, I got a friendly or unfriendly "no," and some doors slammed in my face, and some dogs barking and chasing me. By now...I am totally devastated—and not one listing to show for all my efforts.

I went back to the office, feeling depressed and like an absolute loser. I was so worried because I felt that I was a failure and that people (especially family and friends) would look down on me. This was a reminder of my meager childhood. I could lose my home, my car, etc. What do I do now? I kept wondering if the "Pear Tree Principle" had let me down.

Mr. Kerwin told me to now go out with the other agents in the office and see how they operate. I asked around, but everybody was too busy running to and fro and didn't want to be bothered with a tag along.

I have never failed at anything although I felt I had those close moments. One day, when I was at the office, the owners gave me duty time on the phones. I was thrilled just to talk to a possible buyer or seller. A call came in on a small house in the south area of town that another agent had just listed. Price was only $12,000. It was very old and in an older marginal area. The voice on the phone was a young woman who was just starting out in life and couldn't afford much. I agreed to show her the house the next day. I knew the commission wasn't going to be much, but I had hope in my heart. Next day arrived, and I met with her and her husband. They told me to go ahead and write an offer. I didn't hesitate, as this could be my first sale with this company. Fortunately, the seller accepted the offer and I made a whopping $300 commission! I started to gain a little confidence, but not enough to make a living or to save for more real estate purchases.

Then an idea just struck me. Why should I keep chasing these residential buyers and sellers? Maybe I should focus on investors like I myself have become. Maybe I should start contacting some of them.

So I got in my car and started driving all the streets in my city writing down all addresses that had multiple mailboxes or multiple utility meters or buildings that looked like larger apartment complexes. I then went to the city court house and, using their computer, looked up the ownership of these properties. They told me they had a set of field books that also had multi-dwelling mixed in with residential properties, but I could pick them out of field books if I wished.

I have spent hours and days at the courthouse, and I now had over 6,000 parcels that I derived along with exact addresses and names of owners. I took all these back to the office and began to sort them alphabetically and numerically by street address. Then I looked up each owner's name and phone contact and put them on organized cards.

I then thought, How would I make contact and what would I say? I then wrote a script that I could refer to while I would be on the phone. The script went something like this, "Hello, Mr. Jones…this is Mary Schon with RE Associates real estate company. I specialize in multi-family investment property, and I found your name in the public records as owning a property at 1234 Main Street. Looks like a very nice six plex. Do you think you would be interested in selling if I got you a price that would make you happy?"

Of course, I couldn't read this like a canned speech. I had to put the human element into it and approach it in a relaxed manner.

My first call was to a Mr. Brousseau who said another realtor had previously listed his property and didn't get the job done. This was a seven plex, and I asked him for a chance to market it, but he was very negative and told me that he wasn't interested in listing it again. I proceeded to call the guy back at least six or seven more times, because I knew he wanted to sell but was disappointed in the last realtor. So finally after the last call I made, he said, "Lady, I'm going to give you the listing just to get you off my back." So I got the listing. Well, guess what? I advertised it, and sold it within two weeks.

CHAPTER 25

TIME TO BUILD CONFIDENCE

My confidence was mounting, and I started calling people in large numbers. I was getting so many listings it was unbelievable. At one point I had forty-three listings and many sales pending. So now the rookie was doing sizeable business, and many of the other agents were amazed and took note of this success. I was not only paying my bills now, but had leftover money for new ventures.

Again, the "Pear Tree Principle" kicked in by taking another wild idea, at no cost to me, and capitalizing on it.

We had sales meetings once a month, and at each meeting an award was given (honorary plaque) to the agent who brought in the most listings and the most sales. I was winning plaques consistently. I simply took an avenue that no one else was working and worked it very hard. The income was great, and suddenly I thought the old boss I had at the newspaper actually did me a favor.

I began to know and associate with a lot of investors and discovered that these people bought multiple times, unlike single-family homeowners who you wouldn't see again for another five or ten years. This was a booming business, and I had no investment in it, except time. People kept coming back to me multiple times for more purchases.

Since I had done some income tax work previously part-time at H&R Block, I knew enough to be dangerous and teach people how to defer taxes by 1031 exchanges and other tax-saving methods. This gave them more reason to purchase or sell through me.

Other agents were watching my style and started to pick up some of my business during office-duty phone time. So...I decided, after three years, to leave and start my own company. I began to look for a location but couldn't afford most of the expensive commercial spots and didn't want to engage in a long-term lease.

Then I got another brainstorm. I happened to own an apartment building on a main street in Omaha where there was high traffic count and visibility and good parking. So I cleared the tenants out of the units on the main floor and got 1,500-square feet that I turned into my office space. The second floor still contained two rental units that continued to give me income. Next, I purchased furniture and equipment and officially opened my new company in June of 1980. I named the company Multi-Vest Realty, which was appropriate for what type of business I was doing. My investors all followed me, and now I could keep more of my commission since I didn't have to share it with my former company.

My company thrived for thirty-eight years and is still thriving. Dale H., my old friend, joined me in the company and then eventually started his own property management company. I didn't particularly care for the property management part of the business as much as I liked brokerage and sales. I found that managing my own holdings was as much management as I cared to do. Dealing with multiple tenants and owners and vendors is very time-consuming and quite stressful, while brokerage and sales pay well, with less continual stress.

You see, this type of sales job pays very well and there's a reason for that. Most sales people already have a product to sell, but us realtors have to go out and get our product (the listing) by selling ourselves and our company to clients that will give us the product. Then, we have to sell the listing. So in essence, we have a double-sales job.

But then, I really enjoy sales, going all the way back to my Pear Tree and potholder days. I have no problem talking to strangers as my belief is "every stranger is a friend I haven't met yet."

I found the important thing in this business is to obtain the listing. Listings are gold, and they are the base of this business. Because whether I sell it or another realtor sells it, I still get to go to the bank. It is best if you can sell your own listings, of course.

In order to do any business whatsoever, people have to like you and trust you. You must be genuine and sincere with all your clients and customers. A client is someone you represent. We, realtors, have our customers sign an agency agreement with us, so everybody knows who's working for who. You can represent the seller or the buyer, or you can be a dual agent.

I like representing the seller, as he is generally the one who pays me my commission, and most of my buyers are unrepresented, and I call them customers. Take an example of a sales person sitting at a desk at a car dealership. He represents the dealership, and if you go in to try to buy a car, you are not represented by anyone. You are a customer. That is the best way I can describe how I deal with agency.

Now if a customer has a question or legal problem in a transaction and needs assistance or wants representation in a matter, I refer him to his attorney. It is important with clients and customers to always be in touch. You should return every call or text you receive promptly. Do not delay or your client or customer will go and do business somewhere else. Follow up at all times and also be in touch with all bankers, inspectors, appraisers, title companies, etc., in your transactions.

Never put things off. That is the biggest mistake that most people make. They procrastinate, and then they lose the client or transaction. Be diligent when writing contracts, as they are legal and binding instruments.

Generally speaking, when you write a contract for a customer or if you are writing it for yourself, you should always include some key items.

Be sure you have the correct legal description and address, the total amount of the offer and whether it's going to be all cash or bank- or seller-financed. You should also state any personal property included such as stoves, refrigerators, window air conditioners, etc., as these items are not part of the real estate, unless they are built-in.

If monthly rents are coming in, you should use this phrase in your contract: "Rents to be treated as current and prorated as of day of closing." Some sellers have the notion that they don't have to pro-rate rents they haven't collected yet, and they are absolutely incorrect on this. Rents have to be treated as though they were collected, regardless. And all tenant security deposits are to be transferred to the new buyer.

When writing a contract, you should always make it subject to a full inspection and approval of any and all units and building components. Remember, you can inspect it until the cows come home, but it doesn't mean that you approve. A deadline should be placed in the contract for this due diligence and inspection, or the transaction could go on indefinitely.

Collect a decent earnest deposit from your customer or buyer, to show good faith and consideration and to take the property off the market for any other buyers. I recommend at least $1,000 for every $100,000 of purchase price.

If there are two or more offers on a property at the same time and especially if they are either identical or close in price, go back to both parties and ask them to write their very best offer. It is important that you submit all offers by law to the seller.

Remember also that the seller shouldn't counter both offers, because if each buyer would accept, the seller only has one property to sell. It is best that you have a good lender in your pocket to refer your customers to. Many lenders will only do residential loans, so you have to sort out and find the ones that make multi-family and commercial loans.

You must also find an appraiser that is acceptable to the bank. Sometimes banks have lists of appraisers who they seek bids from. It is not always possible to select your own appraiser. Appraisals are one man's opinion of the market at one moment in time. They are expensive and only good for approximately six months. The appraiser can either make or break your deal, and that is why it is important to provide him or her with all the information necessary that is pertinent to the property, namely the purchase agreement, rent rolls, other income and expenses, and capital improvements. Also try to give him information on other similar recent sales he can compare to. You should also select a good title company to handle your closing and stay in close contact with the key person or persons in charge of your transaction.

Prior to closing, you should make sure that utilities that need to be transferred into the buyer's name and any other services such as trash (dumpster) pickup, coin-operated laundry equipment, lawn services, etc. Every detail must be tended to in order to make a smooth transaction.

When your customers and clients see how well you handled everything, they will definitely want to use your services in the future. Always be diligent and honest and gain their trust.

CHAPTER 26

ESSENTIALS TO NOURISH YOUR PEAR TREE

I've compiled a list of what I believe are the essentials to assure that you will succeed on the path to success and wealth:

1. Choosing the right path
2. Being consistent
3. Perseverance
4. Integrity
5. Discipline and Focus
6. Associate yourself with successful people
7. Learn from your mistakes as well as others
8. Investigate everything before you make decisions
9. Set goals and evaluate yourself and examine your goals
10. Follow up on all issues
11. Always repeat successful performance
12. Keep commitments
13. Utilize training and education
14. Communication is vital
15. Be effective
16. Put forth maximum effort
17. Always be loyal
18. Examine priorities (first things first)

19. Always be responsible
20. Be mature and genuine
21. Take initiative—make things happen
22. Establish sound banking relationships
23. Be enthusiastic
24. Look for opportunities
25. Determination is your friend
26. Be persistent
27. Power of good decision
28. Willpower
29. Thought backed up by strong desire
30. Always utilize strength and power
31. Utilize good habits
32. Be confident, *not* arrogant
33. Use imagination to your advantage (visualize)
34. Be organized
35. Always have courage
36. Do more than needed (go the extra mile)
37. Have understanding
38. Master detail
39. Co-operate with others
40. Utilize self-control
41. Never quit
42. Acquire the burning desire of winning
43. Always translate your ideas into cash
44. Remember there are no limitations to the mind
45. Visualize and believe
46. Utilize the power of thought
47. Think credibility
48. Build multiple pyramids
49. Be a leader, instead of a follower
50. Negotiate everything
51. Take control of the situation

CHAPTER 27

NEGATIVE THINGS THAT WILL PROMOTE FAILURE AND DEATH OF YOUR PEAR TREE

I have also compiled a list of negative things that you should avoid, lest your pear tree will wither and die. They are listed as follows:

1. Fear of failure
2. Lack of ambition
3. Procrastination
4. Being negative
5. Out-of-control spending
6. Inability to co-operate with others
7. Dishonesty
8. Pride and self-righteousness
9. Snap judgments rather than getting the facts
10. Giving up at first sign of opposition
11. Selfishness
12. Lack of organization
13. Wasting time
14. Lack of concentration and determination
15. Being irresponsible
16. Lack of integrity

17. Failure to make and save money
18. Noncommunicative
19. Undisciplined
20. Out-of-line priorities
21. Blaming others

IMPLEMENTING A RESIDENT SEARCH PROGRAM

This type of business is a continual repeat and therefore will give you a constant income month after month as long as you wish.

Your clients who desperately need your service will continue to seek you out and pay you handsomely!

This secret has not been duplicated as far as I know, and if followed properly, you will be in charge of your destiny and enjoy long term financial success.

You *do not* need a cash investment. There is *no* product to sell, no franchise, no multi-level or pyramiding schemes, no mail order, and no product inventory to keep.

If you can pick up a phone and alphabetize names, you can begin "Phase I" of this operation today. Imagine going to your mailbox and receiving countless checks for doing practically nothing. Another "Pear Tree Principle" idea at work. There is no hard physical labor involved. This operation strictly deals in numbers and the more people you service, the wealthier you become.

As a landlord, I quickly became aware of the problems that most landlords face…and that is collection problems from non-paying tenants and evictions resulting from the inability to collect. So now I, as a landlord and property owner, must make a decision. That decision is going to be this: Do I continue to try to work with this person and accept payments in bits and pieces, or am I going to file eviction?

If I file eviction, I will have the cost of court and attorney fees and, of course, the amount of already lost rent plus the stress of coping with the situation.

The sad thing is this: The moment I evict this parasite, he will be out in the streets seeking to rent from a new, unsuspecting landlord, and as you have already guessed, history repeats itself as our deadbeat victimizes *another* landlord.

Who can *stop* this? You say screening more properly on the tenant's application? Wrong! Anyone who has been evicted is embarrassed to admit it. They will, in most cases, lie and falsify an application rather than admit to having been evicted.

After losing much time and thousands of dollars in lost rents, I decided that there must be an easier, fool-proof method of singling out these undesirable tenants once and for all!

One day as I was paying a visit to my attorney's office and while waiting in the reception area, my eyes fell on some magazines and papers sitting on the book stand. More specifically, I picked up a small newspaper entitled the *Daily Record* which is the legal newspaper in my city. As I glanced at it quickly, I skimmed over information regarding court cases, foreclosures, new deeds, mortgages recorded, and lo and behold, "Wrongful Detention of Rent" suits.

I couldn't believe my eyes—there it was in black and white—each and every tenant being sued for non-payment of rent today in my city! Holy Toledo! I thought this is a daily paper. This information is GOLD and can be obtained on a daily basis.

Upon coming back to my office that afternoon, the idea kept running through my mind until I finally decided to call the *Daily Record* newspaper and became a subscriber.

After subscribing and upon receiving my daily copy, I would take a highlighter marker pen and mark each and every new suit for wrongful detention of rent. After doing this, I decided that I would build up a list of these people evicted, and for simplicity's sake, it made sense to do it alphabetically.

I was now prepared to run my own personal check on new applicants who wanted to rent an apartment from me. As this list continued to grow, more and more bad tenant names were entered until I had a substantial list. At this point, the number was so great, it was necessary to put them into a computer.

You absolutely wouldn't believe how many times I had been contacted by one of these deadbeats that were already on this list—seeking to rent from me. Many of them owed hundreds, if not thousands, to their former landlords.

Imagine, had I rented to these people, my losses would be definitely enhanced. Tenants who were exposed to this were appalled and baffled that I should even be aware of such information about them. Confronting an applicant with this information is like seeing him with egg all over his face.

Now...I am aware that it may not seem legal or kosher to maintain a bad list of people which is self-developed; however, this method is perfectly legal since it is already of public record. These were actual case filings as each had reference to it by a docket and case numbers filed with the county court. What I am doing is simply accumulating and dispensing information and acting as a reference agent with current accurate files.

The idea worked so well for me that I decided that it would be valuable as well to other landlords. Since I was already in real estate and knew several landlords in the city, my mere mention of this idea got them very excited. Most agreed that they were too busy to develop a list like that but would be willing to pay for that information. This is all that I needed to fulfill a real need and to make profit at the same time. And at this point, it seemed the proper thing to do is to make this service available and to get organized.

HOW TO IMPLEMENT THE IDEA

The first step is to always have an active current list of the evictions on a daily basis in your file. In your case, if you want to do this, you will not have one or two years of information in front of you immediately. You are going to have to do some research. If you know of the daily legal paper in your area, you should subscribe immediately. To obtain previous eviction notices, you must ask the paper for old copies of the paper or old issues that may be on microfilm in their library. Most newspapers keep old copies of each issue or have old issues on microfilm. This may take a while to do, but it is obviously worth it.

The next task is to spend some time compiling these names. When you do this, be sure to go back one or two years to ensure you have accumulated a list of value. Also include the name of the landlord or management company doing the eviction and of the dollar amount owed if shown. Be careful to spell all names correctly and get middle initials where possible. For instance, you could be more specific when you list John Doe as John R. Doe. This saves confusion in identity if there happens to be two John Does in the city. If you are able to obtain a social security number, that's even better. One thing is for sure is that you can check with the former landlord if there is any reason at all for confusion of identity.

At this point you have the back issues researched, and you are adding new names from your current source daily to your list. Now is the time to make your efforts pay off handsomely!

Since most landlords at this point would probably just be dying to have your list, you have a *valuable product. Do not sell the product!* I repeat, *do not, under any circumstances, sell your compiled list.*

If you sell it to one landlord, be assured it will be duplicated and distributed throughout the rental community, who will then in turn not be as willing to subscribe to your service. Besides, new evictions are being added every day. That is why it is imperative that you market this information as a service instead of a product. This service is an on-going, up-to-date entity and will give you income month after month as long as you care to continue to offer it.

I will describe the procedure for setup in the next few pages, but first let me say that nothing is valuable unless someone gives it value and that someone is willing to pay a fee for that information or service. Prices have always been set worldwide on a supply-and-demand basis. In your area, no matter where you live, there is a dormant demand for this information. It is dormant only because it has never been developed and marketed. The problem it solves has always existed, but the answer to that problem has not been found until now.

At this point you may say, "I don't personally know any landlords. How do I go about finding those in my community that will want to buy my service?"

First of all, go to your local daily paper and open it to the classified section where there are listings of "Apartments and houses for rent." Jot down these phone numbers and cross-reference them through a city directory or cross directory in order to obtain the landlord or complex name. If you don't have a city directory, you can use one at your public library. Often, phone companies will rent cross directories to customers for a nominal fee. City directories and cross directories also show what properties are multi-dwelling. If you have the address, simply punch it into the computer at the local court house and the owner/landlord's name will appear.

You can also go to your local court house and go through their field books or computer system in order to pull up names and property addresses of multi-family dwellings. You already have a set of names from your first list of landlords who filed suits for wrongful detention of rent from your bad tenant list and these people are prime candidates and excellent sources of "would be" customers.

You may even place a small classified ad under the investment section of your local paper appealing to landlords who could utilize your service. The personal services column may also be another avenue to explore.

Whatever way or ways you choose to do this, you should come up with several hundred or even thousands of landlords and management companies if you live in or near a metropolitan area. It is important that you gather as many landlord and management company names as possible. Each one is a potential perpetual income to you.

When calling on these people, take your accumulated list of deadbeats and total for them the ones they had evicted last year and the cost per person they had to sue for, as this is a strong sales tool for new subscriptions to your service. Show them you could have saved them *big dollars* had they belonged to your service.

You must continue now with perseverance, enthusiasm, and a positive mental attitude. Now that you have a substantial list of landlords and property management companies and phone numbers, you must formulate your plan of attack. By that, I mean you must prepare a presentation that will excite these landlords into becoming your client. Your service should be inexpensive so that all can afford it and you can attract clients in large numbers. Many years ago when I started, I offered landlords membership for a mere $10 per month. This fee included three free inquiries and with additional inquiries beyond the limitation at just fifty cents each.

Today, I am sure you could charge more than when I first implemented the program and still make it reasonable to attract many clients. The reason the cost was low was to build volume. If someone had only ten or twelve units, he's not overpaying for the service, but if he or a company has two hundred to five hundred units, he/they will be charged as a heavier user. So it ends up being fair to everyone. Next, you should set up a special phone line. I suggest putting in a second line or teen line which is far less expensive than connecting a business phone. I used an unpublished phone number for privacy and I used self-sticking bright colored labels that I gave out to my clients to affix to their phones that contained my private phone number on, so they would always have my number handy when they were ready to make an inquiry. The sticker also contained a privacy code that I assigned to each landlord account. For instance, if the landlord's last name was Adams (which starts with A) and he was the fifth person with the last initial A that became a client, his secret code would be A-5. The reason for this is that if someone called in for inquiries misrepresenting his identity, the landlords account of inquiries would not be charged. And billing is easier if everything is kept track of by account number identity. Everyone paid for exactly as much usage as he/they ordered. No one was allowed to cheat or infringe on another client's account.

An example copy of my self-sticking phone number and code identification are featured in this chapter. You should have these printed in an attention-getting color, using bold numerals for your phone number and company name.

Your choice of company name should be compatible with the type of business you represent. Your name must project your image. For instance, I called my company "Resident Search," but you can call yourself or company anything you like. Just let your imagination run wild as long as it does not infringe on the name of another existing business or company.

When a client calls in and gives you the name of his prospective tenant, you check it against your referenced bad list and report *only* what is of public record. Never give a personal opinion or recommendation. You may name the last landlord that evicted the tenant, the date of record, the case number, and the amount of rent sued for if available. You are not breaking any privacy laws as this is a matter of *public record.*

Normally, I list all new suits filed whether or not they have actually ended up in final eviction and judgment. At least one thing is certain, there was a definite rent collection problem. If on a later date a dismissal or judgment is entered, it would be a good idea to note that. Sometimes a dismissal could mean that the tenant moved out before court date, and the landlord himself therefore did not show up for court. In this case, a dismissal is entered, but this does *not* mean that there wasn't a problem originally.

After you get a numerous amount of names, you may want to use word-processing to alphabetize them on the computer. You will also want to back up your computer information frequently if not daily. This system also enhances your speed in referencing. It is highly recommended when your list begins to grow.

You may then ask yourself, How much money can I make doing this? It all depends on you. The major job you will have is contacting hundreds of landlords and management companies and explaining the benefits of this program. I suggest a personal phone call or visit, as mail outs are costly and not totally proven effective. You can accumulate a solid and sound monthly base and add to it by the individual overages every month. Most of my accounts spent substantially more per month on overages than on the base membership fee.

The cost of monthly and annual membership more than pays for itself in savings to the landlord from even at least one bad tenant. This must be part of your sales presentation. The landlord simply can't afford to be without your service. And besides, you can explain to the landlords and companies that your service is *tax deductible* to them.

And this is a more than 90 to 95 percent profitable business to you. You have everything to gain and nothing to lose. And a further savings suggestion I will make to you is that you can save on postage and time by billing quarterly instead of monthly.

This, indeed, is another spin-off of the "Pear Tree Principle."

Resident Search
345-1346
(A Private Screening Source)
Your Code #

This type of self-sticking label should be provided to the land-lord or property manager to affix to his phone so as to provide easy access to your service. An area shown above to be blank can be used to insert a privacy code number. Remember to have this label printed in a bright, attention-getting color.

MARY E. SCHON

LIST OF LEGAL NEWSPAPERS
THROUGHOUT THE UNITED STATES

Index of Court, Legal, Business, Commercial, and Financial Newspapers

California
Daily Commerce
915 E 1st Street
Los Angeles, CA 90012-4050
(213)229-5300

Metropolitan News
210 S Spring Street
Los Angeles, CA 90012
(213)346-0033

Inter-City Express
1109 Oak Street, #103
Oakland, CA 94607
(510)272-4747

Wall Street Journal
1701 Page Mill Rd.
Palo Alto, CA 94304
(650)493-2800

The Daily Recorder
901 H Street, #312
Sacramento, CA 95814
(916)444-2355

The Transcript
2nd floor, 2625 Fourth Ave.
San Diego, CA 92103
(619)232-3486

Recorder
1035 Market Street
San Francisco, CA 94103
(415)490-9990

San Jose Post Record
95 S Market St., #535
San Jose, CA 95113
(408)287-4866

Colorado
Transcript
235 S Nevada Ave
Colorado Springs, CO 80903
(719)634-5905

Illinois
Chicago Daily Law Bulletin
415 N State Street
Chicago, IL 60610
(312)644-7800

Iowa
Business Record
100 SW 4th Street
Des Moines, IA 50309
(515)288-3336

Kansas
Wichita Journal
121 N Mead, #100
Wichita, KS 67202
(316)267-6406

Louisiana
Daily Legal News
501 Texas Street, Ste. #M103
Shreveport, LA 71101
(318)222-0213

Maryland
The Daily Record
200 St. Paul Pl., #2480
Baltimore, MD 21202
(443)524-8100

Michigan
Detroit Legal News Publishing
1409 Allen Dr., #B
Troy, MI 48226
(248)577-6100

Minnesota
Saint Paul Legal Ledger
332 N Minnesota Street,
#W-1293
St. Paul, MN 55101
(612)584-1563

Missouri
Countian
7733 Forsyth Blvd.
Clayton, MO 63105
(314)727-6111

Daily Record
920 Main Street, #825
Kansas City, MO 64106
(816)931-2002

Daily Events Co.
310 W. Walnut Street
Springfield, MO 65806
(417)866-1401

St. Joseph Daily Courier
1020 S 10th Street
St. Joseph, MO 64503
(816)279-3441

Missouri Lawyers Weekly
319 N Fourth Street, 5th floor
St. Louis, MO 63102
(314)412-1880

Nebraska
Daily Record
3323 Leavenworth Street
Omaha, NE 68105
(402)345-1303

New York
American Banker
One State Street Plaza
1 Whitehall Street
New York, NY 10004
(212)803-8200

The Daily Record
16 W Main Street
Rochester, NY 14614
(585)232-6920

Ohio

Akron Legal News
60 S Summit Street
Akron, OH 44308
(330)376-0917

Cincinnati Press
119 W Central Pkwy., #2
Cincinnati, OH 45202
(513)241-1450

CHAPTER 29

Expand Your Horizons

Now that your business is running smoothly and you have many satisfied customers, you may want to look at expanding in an additional direction. In most cases, you will have prevented these owners from renting to a bad tenant of record, but there is a remote chance that a landlord may rent to a first-time offender or someone who has never been exposed by court records. Perhaps he's a new resident to your community. You can still be of assistance to your landlords.

There is a method of eviction called *pro-se,* which I have mentioned in an earlier chapter. What that means is that the landlord may act as his own attorney in eviction court if he personally owns the property. He simply files his own petition and praecipe and is present on the designated court date to be granted restitution.

The process is somewhat involved, and most landlords, because of unfamiliarity with the procedure, turn this task over to their attorneys. These attorneys, who of course are proving their worth and trying to make a good living, will charge $300 to $500 per eviction plus court costs and filing fees. Can you see how expensive this can get for the landlord? He's already owed several hundred dollars from the deadbeat tenant he's throwing out, and now he has to pay another $300 or more to hire an attorney to get rid of him.

Frankly, I learned the hard way. After spending hundreds of dollars in attorney fees, a friend of mine tipped me off that she was using a standardized petition form drawn up by an attorney with certain areas left blank to fill in and a praecipe provided by the filing desk clerk, and her costs were less than $40 per eviction. She gave me step-by-step instructions as to how to proceed with the eviction by myself, and I've been doing it ever since and have saved thousands of dollars over the years. A sample of my petition and praecipe are shown in this book as a typical example of the form you need to fill out to proceed with your eviction.

My petition has two causes of action. The first cause of action is for restitution (which means physical repossession of the property or unit), and the second cause of action is for monetary damages. What you need to do is to find out all you can about the *pro-se* evictions in your community. Compile a step-by-step instruction booklet and standardized forms that the landlord can simply fill in. You may want to seek the help of the staff at the filing desk of your municipal or county court and interview at least two or three attorneys about the procedure in your area.

It is against the law for you to do this for anyone else except yourself, because you can be accused of practicing law without a license. Even if you own a company, corporation, LLC, etc., you cannot act in their behalf as you can only act in behalf of yourself. But you can teach others how they can act for themselves by creating a self-help booklet and charging for the booklet.

Make up complete eviction packets with instructions and offer them to people on your landlord list for a nominal fee such as $35 to $50. Landlords will love you for this, for you are again saving them hundreds of dollars while gaining their friendship and loyalty. In fact, most of them will consider you a hero deserving of an accommodation.

You should provide blank forms for use by the purchaser of your kit when following your instruction booklet. The whole eviction proceeding should be in one complete packet. And remember... once an eviction is filed, the tenants name goes onto the deadbeat list that you are also forming.

One more thing you can recommend to your landlords is that after the eviction and monetary judgments have been established by the judge, your landlords can take the court judgment and turn it over to a collection agency so that the collection agency can continue to dog these people and garnish their future wages and return some of this money to the landlord. Generally, they will split their collection on fifty-fifty basis with the landlord.

Example Forms

- **Official 3 day notice to pay or quit**
- **Eviction Praecipe**
- **Eviction petition**
- **Estoppel Agreement**

OFFICIAL
NOTICE TO PAY OR QUIT
RENT IN ARREARS

TO: _____

_____

_____

Subject to the conditions set forth below, you are hereby notified to **leave the premises** now occupied by you at _____, in Omaha, Douglas County, Nebraska, and deliver possession of same to the undersigned within **3 days of this notice**.

FOR THE MONTH   OF   AMOUNT DUE   FEES

If the amount of $_____is paid within 3 days of the date of this notice, this notice will become void.

Dated this_____day of _____,20___

_____

By_____

CERTIFICATION

I hereby ceritify that on this____day of_____,20____notice was served by me upon_____
_____ at _____
_____, Omaha,Nebraska by leaving/mailing a copy at the address set forth above.

_____

STATE OF NEBRASKA	**PRAECIPE**	
C/SC 123 (6/96)		

Douglas County Court, Civil/Small Claims Division
1819 Farnam Street, Farnam Level, Omaha, NE 68183 (402) 444-5424

_____ Plaintiff,
vs.   PRAECIPE

_____
Defendant.   Case No. _____

To the Clerk of said Court:

Please issue _____

_____

_____

_____

_____

_____

_____

in the above entitled cause.

DATE: _____ PRO SE'S/
ATTORNEY'S SIGNATURE: _____

ATTORNEY NUMBER: _____

ADDRESS: _____

CITY, STATE, ZIP CODE: _____

TELEPHONE NUMBER: _____

SAMPLE

IN THE COUNTY COURT OF
DOUGLAS COUNTY, NEBRASKA

	)	DOC. NO.
	)	
	)	
	)	
Plaintiff/s	)	
	)	
	)	**PETITION**
Vs.	)	
	)	
	)	
Defendant/s	)	

FIRST CAUSE OF ACTION

COMES NOW The plaintiff/s on _____and for His/her/their First Cause of Action against the defendant/s, allege/s and state/s as follows:

I.

That the plaintiff/s and the defendant/s are residents of Omaha, Douglas County, Nebraska.

II.

That the plaintiff/s are the owners of the following real property:_____ _____Omaha, Douglas County, Nebraska

III.

That the defendant/s occupy the premises as tenant/s pursuant to a rental Agreement.

IV.

That the defendant/s has/have failed to pay the rent due for _____ _____ 20____, in the amount of $ _____

V.

That on the _____day of_____, 20____, the plaintiff/s served a notice for termination of rental agreement for non-payment of rent upon the defendant/s requesting Him/her /them to vacate said premises, but the defendant/s has/have failed to do so as requested in said notice and is/are unlawfully and forcibly holding possession of said property notwithstanding said notice.

WHEREFORE, plaintiff/s pray/s for a judgment of restitution on his/her/their First Cause Action, together with his/her/their costs herein expended.

SECOND CAUSE OF ACTION

COMES NOW the plaintiff/s and for his/her/their Second Cause of Action against The defendant/s allege/s as follows:

I.

The plaintiff/s incorporate/s paragraph I, II and III of his/her/their First Cause Of Action as fully as though set out herein.

II.

That the agreed rental was _____; that defendant/s Has/have failed to pay said rent for _____ 20_____.

That the plaintiff/s ha/have requested defendant/s to pay the rent, but defendant/s has/have refused to do so and continue to do so.

WHEREFORE, plaintiff/s pray/s for a judgment against the defendant/s in his/her/their Second Cause of Action in the amount of $ _____, plus a reasonable amount for his/her/their costs herein expended.

_____

_____
Plaintiff/s.

TENANT ESTOPPEL CERTIFICATE

Date: _____, 20__ at _____
FACTS:
1. This certificate pertains to terms and conditions under the following lease agreement:
   1.1 dated_____, 20__, at _____
   1.2 entered into by_____, as the Landlord, and
   1.3 _____, as the Tenant,
   1.4 regarding real estate referred to as Apartment # _____, _____Apartments
STATEMENT:
Tenant certifies as follows:
2. The lease agreement is:
   ( ) Unmodified and in effect.
   ( ) Modified and in effect under a modification agreement dated _____, 20__
3. Tenant is in possession of the premises, and has not assigned or sublet any portion of the premises, except_____
4. The current term of the lease commenced on _____, 20__
5. The term of the lease shall expire on _____, 20__
6. The amount of the monthly rent is _____.
7. The amount of Security Deposit is $_____.
8. No breach of the agreement by Landlord or Tenant presently exists, except:
_____
9. Tenant has caused no lien or encumbrance to attach to the leasehold interest in the property.
10. Tenant understands this certificate will be relied on by a buyer of the property or a Lender secured by the real estate.

11.   I certify the above is true and correct
     Date: _____, 20__

     Tenant's Name _____

     Signature: _____

     Phone: _____

CHAPTER 30

AND THERE'S EVEN MORE

G ood luck and fortune never stop coming your way as success
is parked at your doorstep. Your new sought- after ambitions
have kept you very busy, but not too busy to enjoy still another clever
benefit of this profitable program. You have by now accumulated a
huge list of property owners and landlords and have come to know
many of them personally. You have done a great deal of business with
them, and they have grown to like you and trust you.

Other people in various fields would just love to get their hands
on this landlord list, wouldn't they? Why? Because it is golden. I
remember when I was new in the real estate business and decided to
specialize in selling multi-family dwellings. I made it a point to get
every single multi-family dwelling in my city and the owner of each
one typed on a three-by-five-inch reference card. This took a consid-
erable amount of time, but I obtained numerous listings from these
contacts. I would have loved to have bought a list instead of accumu-
lating data the hard way. It would have shortened the research time.

However, now you already have quite a bit of this information
in your database. This information is valuable to other people such
as realtors (to obtain listings) or insurance agents (to sell insurance)
or laundry machine equipment companies that place their washers
and dryers in landlords' buildings. Hardware stores may also be able
to use this information as they send out flyers to customers who need

their merchandise. Heating, air-conditioning, plumbing companies, and electrical companies may also have need for such a list. Other service industries may also buy your list. Selling mailing lists can be quite profitable, and what's more, they can be sold over and over again to more than one company. The profit potential here is absolutely staggering!

You only need to implement one of my ideas in order to make a sizeable profit, but if you are aggressive and profit-conscious, you will probably add on additional services. Remember, the more services you offer, the more organized you will need to be, and the more money you will make.

Again…the "Pear Tree Principle" proven and working!

CHAPTER 31

--- ❀ ---

ONE MORE HOT TIP

If you have or can obtain a real estate license in your locality, you may profit from one more aspect of this lucrative business. As a rule, licensed people, either brokers or those under the direction of a broker, may collect a commission fee for either management or the renting out of a unit. This bonus is usually a percentage of the first month's rent. Generally, 50 percent is common.

If the rental unit is vacant and costing the landlord money, you can find a renter and collect one-half of his first month's rent for yourself and at the same time help the landlord fill the vacancy. Most full-fledged management companies not only rent out the units, but also pay all the incoming bills and take care of all the service calls and give a monthly monetary accounting to the owner.

If you feel you are not interested in the day-to-day operation of apartment buildings and houses but strictly want to act as a rental agent, you may obtain listings of vacant units with all data and set of keys from the landlords, who in turn will sign a rental contract with you agreeing to pay you 50 percent of the first month's rent or 50 percent of the deposit for each unit you fill.

You then run a general ad for apartments for rent using a cumulative list of all the combined units that the landlords have listed with you. In other words, you can obtain listings of units for rent from several landlords and act as a rental/leasing agent for each of them. This also can be *very* lucrative.

As I mentioned, you *must* have a real estate license in your state for doing this, unless you are a resident manager in the landlord's building and he is paying you as an employee, or you are breaking the law.

And as long as you now have your real estate license, you could eventually obtain property listings "for sale" from your list of land-lords. After all, by now, they like and trust you.

Commissions on such sales of apartment buildings and duplexes generally range between 5 to 8 percent of the gross-sale price. Therefore, if you listed and sold an apartment building for say $100,000 and the commission rate was 7 percent, you just made a cool $7,000 commission. Not bad for one transaction!

One thing I can honestly say about selling investment prop-erty is that the buyer generally is not as picky as a home buyer. He normally doesn't care about how large the bedrooms are or what color the carpet is. He's mostly interested in the amount of income it brings in and the positive cash flow to him after debt service. If you can meet this criteria, be assured you will obtain future business. Investment property is by far the easiest property to sell, as you are selling an income and tax shelter. Along with these benefits are equity buildup and further borrowing potential. Most people, by nature, are attracted by greed and this commodity certainly fills the bill.

One more thought to bear in mind is that if you act as a realtor working on a property of this type, you will not have to hold open houses, which are very time-consuming. Your Sundays will be freed up to spend as you choose with your family and friends. Also, the turn-around period for re-sell of this type property is much faster. If you sell a single-family home, chances are you won't see these folks again until they decide to step up or step down in probably five to ten years when they might get ready to move again. However, with investment property, you can expect that a landlord will resell gen-erally somewhere between one to three years, or he may decide to add to his portfolio and buy additional property and add to what he already has.

Each time he gets involved in a transaction you generate, you get paid a handsome commission. Many of my landlord owners have purchased four and five and as many as ten buildings from me within a year or two.

If you, as a realtor, are involved in a two- or three-way exchange, all parties in the transaction will be paying you individually a commission. So...*bingo*...it looks like you *win* again! Remember, you *must* be licensed to do this phase of activity. In order to obtain a license (which we talked about in a former chapter), you must check the requirements of your particular state and qualify by generally taking a state board exam. Many times there is a minimum period of time required that one must have resided in a particular state before one can even qualify. The test is composed of general real estate knowledge of documents, concept of law, and math relating to sample transactions. A general knowledge of closing statements for both buyer and seller are also required. A portion of the test is also related to State License Law of the particular state you are applying for.

CHAPTER 32

ME, A MILLIONAIRE?

In conclusion, this book and each of the concepts I have revealed to you will not only give you a vast amount of information, but will also make you a tidy profit. As you can readily see, it is now up to you to follow the "Pear Tree Principle" and to implement one or more of the phases that will begin to generate wealth and success and start you on the path to financial freedom.

You will have groundwork to lay, but at least you may start with little or no capital investment, which is a rare opportunity anywhere. Nothing to risk and nowhere to go but *up*! In pursuit of your new goals, you may even be able to think up some additional services that you may add on top of the ones I have already mentioned. The key to success in these ventures is volume. The more landlords you contact, the more services you sell, the more money you make.

You may choose to do just a few of the phases and choose not to become licensed, or you may become licensed and enjoy all the benefits of this entire book. You may decide to work any and all of these phases either full-time or part-time, but be assured that the more time you spend on each phase, the more money you will make.

It is not inconceivable to earn $3,000 to $15,000 or more per month on just *one* phase of this operation and much more if you try hard and implement several of the phases. The progress of your operation is entirely up to *you*.

I have given you all the necessary tools to get started. You must nourish your own "**PEAR TREE**," and in turn add the ingredients of enthusiasm, consistency, perseverance, and persistence, and you *will* indeed be well on your way to enjoying your new *millionaire status*!

And always remember, "You can't have the *fruits* without the *roots*." My *best of luck* to you in your pursuit!

9 781645 845591